BEES, BEEKEEPING, HONEY
AND POLLINATION

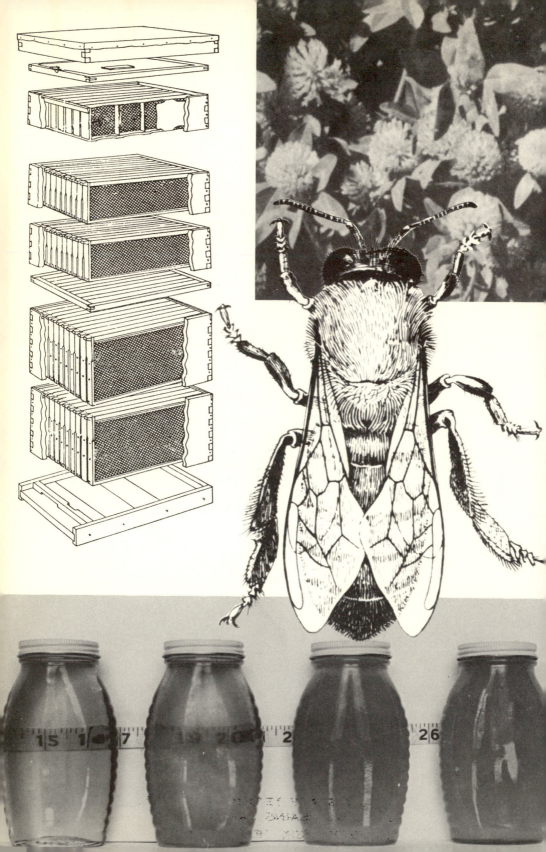

BEES, BEEKEEPING, HONEY AND POLLINATION

Walter L. Gojmerac

Professor of Entomology
University of Wisconsin
Madison, Wisconsin

AVI PUBLISHING COMPANY, INC.
Westport, Connecticut

Library of Congress Cataloging in Publication Data

Gojmerac, Walter L
    Bees, beekeeping, honey, and pollination.

    Includes bibliographies and index.
    1. Bees. 2. Bee culture. I. Title.
SF523.G64   638′.1   79–23348
ISBN 0–87055–342–9

Printed in the United States of America by Eastern Graphics, Inc.,
Old Saybrook, Connecticut

Preface

From recorded history honey bees have been observed, admired, studied, or feared by people. They provided the first, and in many cases, the only sweetener (honey) and probably the first plastic and waterproofing material (beeswax). However, it was only in this last century that people began to realize and appreciate their real value as pollinators of many food and forage crops.

Within the last decade, there has been a dramatic surge of interest in honey bees, ranging from the scientist engaged in the systematic study of bees, to the agriculturist whose food and forage crops require pollination by honey bees, to the plant breeder needing the honey bee for cross pollination, and, finally, to the naturalist furthering his understanding of the environment.

Land Grant Colleges through the Extension Service, as well as suppliers of beekeeping equipment provide excellent and adequate directions on "how to" begin a beekeeping operation explaining such details as purchasing or making equipment, installing packaged bees, and extracting honey. But the *students of beekeeping* today have a diverse background. They may be professionals, technicians, or food producers who need the services of the honey bee, or businessmen, housewives, factory workers or physicians who are interested in a worthwhile, stimulating, and challenging diversion from their chosen occupation. These people want to know why or what is the rationale behind each operation. This not only makes beekeeping more interesting and rewarding, but allows decisions to be made with confidence.

That agriculture has dramatically changed is self-evident. Small diversified farms are being rapidly replaced by large acreages of single crops. The natural habitat of many native pollinators living in the fence rows, hedges, patches of weeds, etc., has been lost or destroyed. The farmer in many cases has no choice other than to utilize honey bees to perform the vital service of pollination.

The merits of honey as a food and medicine have been debated from recorded history. While there are some who maintain that honey has mysterious and/or still undiscovered attributes, everyone agrees that, when handled properly, it is a fine wholesome food, enjoyed by many. While hobbyists generally keep bees to produce honey, the honey bee's value as a pollinator far exceeds the usefulness of honey.

Honey bees have fascinated philosophers, artists, and skillful writers. They also have been studied by serious researchers in academic institutions and government laboratories. These activities resulted in a substantial body of literature—scholarly as well as popularized writings. Unfortunately, some of the popularized versions are not always accurate, and some scholarly reports are in specialized libraries, not readily accessible to interested individuals.

The purpose of this book is to organize a body of information on bees, beekeeping, honey production, and pollination into one coherent package. I have placed minimum emphasis on the "elementary how to" and have concentrated on the why and the rationale behind specific operations. The quantity of literature related to this topic is immense so I have had to be selective in references, citations, and examples. I have tried to explain the basic operations in a manner meaningful to the person without extensive scientific and/or biological training, yet not oversimplify the content to the point where it is meaningless to the more serious beekeeping student.

Many universities teach a course on beekeeping (Apiculture) during the regular session, but a large number of people learn beekeeping by attending evening classes at vocational technical schools, university extension services, or community colleges through continuing education programs. Instructors for these courses do not always have suitable library resources related to bees and beekeeping, or even time to prepare supplementary reading. The "adult" student wants practical, pertinent, and factual information related to the subject being studied.

Based on my training and experience as a beekeeper, entomologist, teacher of beginning beekeeper classes, and organizer of special seminars for beekeeping instructors, I feel that this book will meet the requirements of the instructors and the interests of the students in the area of beekeeping. Adequate references are given so that the student is able to explore in depth any topic of special interest, yet the citations have been kept to a minimum so as not to detract the reader.

I would like to express my appreciation to Dr. Norman W. Desrosier and Ms. Karen L. Carter of the AVI Publishing Company for their encouragement and assistance in bringing this book into being.

WALTER L. GOJMERAC
Madison, Wisconsin

May 1979

Contents

1

Honey Bee and Its Relatives

Whether it was the taste of honey, the pain of a sting, or the sight of a swarm that first attracted man to bees is unknown. However, man has been associated with bees since recorded history. On a subject where there is a long history of popular literature and technical writing, it is important to agree on a precise definition of words and terms for a meaningful discussion. Beekeeping and Apiculture are often used synonymously. However, beekeeping refers to the husbandry of a specific species of insect, *Apis mellifera*; whereas Apiculture is more inclusive, referring to the science dealing with all insects belonging to the family Apidae. The words "bee," "honey bee," and "honeybee" are often used interchangeably. Most dictionaries spell "honey bee" as one word, as do some trade journals, but the Committee on Common Names of Insects of the Entomological Society of America ruled that when a two-part name is used it should be spelled as two separate words. Some examples are house fly, bumble bee, lady beetle, and of course honey bee. Colony and hive are sometimes confused by the non-professional. Colony refers to a group of bees, workers, drones, and a queen, existing as one organized unit. A hive is the home-equipment or structure housing the colony.

A brief summary of insect classification may help the non-entomologist understand the relationship of the honey bee *(Apis mellifera L.)* to the multitude of other insects also including other bees and wasps.

Bees belong to the order Hymenoptera. This is a relatively large and diverse group, and entomologists in general consider it as probably the most beneficial of all orders. While there are some destructive members, the majority are parasitic on destructive insects, predaceous, or serve other useful purposes such as pollination and production of honey and wax. Adult Hymenoptera are recognized by their two pairs of thin membraneous wings, the second pair being smaller than the first. The rear wing is equipped with small hooks (hamuli). In flight this wing attaches to the first so both work as one unit. Hymenoptera undergo complete metamorphosis, and most females have an ovipositor which can

1

be used as a stinger.

The binomial system of classification was developed by Linneaus in 1758. Each living organism was given a genus and species designation. Several genera with similar or related characteristics are grouped into families, families into orders, and orders into classes. These taxonomic groupings in general tend to show phylogenetic or evolutionary relationships. The honey bee belongs to the family Apidae, order Hymenoptera, class Insecta. Due to diversity and complexity of Hymenoptera, taxonomists over the years found it useful to subdivide or group these commonly used designations into sub and super, e.g., subfamily and superfamily. Family names always end in *idae*, superfamily in *oidae*, and subfamily in *inae*. Genus and species names are latinized and in italics.

Taxonomists differ in their practice of grouping categories. Some tend to lump or group organisms rather liberally; others tend to split or divide them into smaller units. For this reason one reference may list 7 or 8 families within one order, while another may have 10 or 15 in that same order. For example, some authors list the bumble bee in the same family as the honey bee—Apidae, while others use a separate family name Bombidae.

Hymenoptera are usually divided into two suborders, ten superfamilies of wasps and one of bees. The number of families of bees varies with the taxonomists, ranging between 6 and 12, with 3 subfamilies in Apidae. Superfamilies of social Hymenoptera and families of bees are summarized in Table 1.1.

TABLE 1.1. SOCIAL HYMENOPTERA

	Common Examples
SUPERFAMILIES	
Scolioidea	Ants and some parasitic wasps
Vespoidea	Paper, potter, and spider wasps
Sphecoidea	Sphecoid wasps and mud dabbers
Apoidea	Bees
FAMILIES OF BEES	
Colletidae	Plasterer and yellow-faced bees
Halictidae	Halictid and alkali bees
Andrenidae	Andrenid bees
Metillidae	Melittid bees
Megachilidae	Leaf-cutting bees
Fideliidae	—
Anthophoridae	Digger and cuckoo bees
Xylocopidae	Carpenter bees
Oxaeidae	Oxaeid bees
Bombidae	Bumble bees (in England, Humble bees)
Apidae	Honey, euglossid and stingless bees

Wasps are a close relative of bees. This is an extremely large and diverse group and generally recognized as more primitive. The majority are solitary. That is, they live alone and not in a community, either

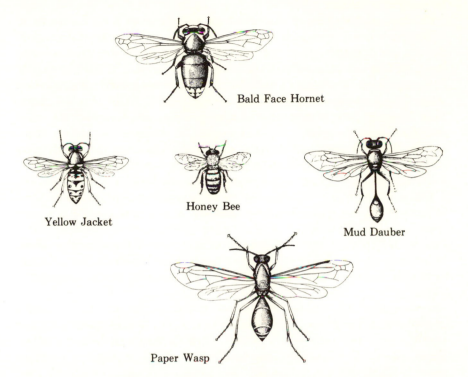

Bald Face Hornet

Yellow Jacket

Honey Bee

Mud Dauber

Paper Wasp

FIG. 1.1. SEVERAL WASPS SOMETIMES MISTAKEN FOR HONEY BEES

parasitic or predaceous, and those that are social do not have the degree of specialization found in the honey bee. Only the fertilized queen survives the winter, and the nest made from bits of wood or cellulose is reconstructed each year. There are two superfamilies of social wasps, Vespoidea and Sphecoidea. Each group builds its own specific kind of nest. Some search out a cavity either above or below ground, others build a free hanging, open nest, while some enclose it in a "paper" envelope. The compartments called cells, in which larvae develop, hang vertically, which differs from the horizontal cells the honey bee builds. The honey bee uses the cells as a nursery to rear young interchangeably with food storage. This adaptation enables the colony to survive through prolonged periods when food is not available. While wasps have a small quantity of body reserves to carry them through periods of stress, the species is perpetuated through the fertilized queen. Workers and males die each fall and the fertilized queen spends the winter in hibernation in some sheltered area. The following season she must select a suitable site for a nest and start the construction process, lay some eggs, and care for the newly hatched larvae. The first born are workers (females) who will help with food gathering and building additions to the nest. As the season progresses the colony numbers increase along with the nest size, and towards mid-summer or early autumn both males and females are produced. Mating occurs between individuals from different colonies, and it is these mated or fertilized queens which provide the next generation.

There are eleven family names of bees listed in Table 1.1, including Apidae, which includes the honey bee. There are four species of honey bees: *A. florea, A. dorsata, A. mellifera,* and *A. indica (cerana). Apis mellifera* is the one that is predominant in the world today. *Apis florea* is referred to as the little honey bee, while *dorsata* is called the giant honey bee. Both are found in Southeast Asia and are considered to be more primitive than *mellifera.* They have a system of communication between workers, but it is not as refined as it is in *mellifera.* Somewhat like wasps, they build a single comb in the open but in a sheltered site. Colonies of *florea* are small by comparison to *mellifera* and *dorsata.* Since the comb is exposed, a large percentage of the workers is relegated to defend the colony from predators. They do not gather and store a large surplus of honey. Since food is available essentially all year, they do not have to store it.

Apis dorsata builds one large comb which may be a meter or more in circumference. It is an exposed comb and it develops a large population. Like *A. florea* it stores little excess honey. *Apis indica,* as the name suggests, is found in India. Some use the name *cerana* to designate this species. This species is used for honey production although quantities stored are quite small compared to *A. mellifera.*

Apis mellifera is of course the remarkable honey bee. It builds nests in cavities and is capable of gathering large quantities of nectar and pollen when conditions are favorable, and stores it for future use. It is primarily because of these characteristics that the honey bee, *Apis mellifera,* is such a successful creature. It has been associated with man since recorded history, transported to all continents and readily adapted to the new environment.

The original homeland of the honey bee, or its immediate ancestor, is believed to be somewhere on the Euro-Asian continent possibly near Southeast Asia or Northern India. As it dispersed, populations became isolated either by distance or by geographic barriers. Whether these populations are subspecies or races is an academic question. Nevertheless, these groups represent different genotypes especially adapted to their environment. Races can be distinguished by color and behavior patterns and by precise measurements of certain morphological structures such as the length of mouth parts, wing venation, and hair patterns. Because of selection and cross breeding in the United States today, no true races exist, even though some genetic lines are distinctly identifiable by behavior and color. The common races are listed in Table 1.2. Some are of academic interest and others serve as gene pools for breeding stock.

TABLE 1.2. RACES OF BEES

Latin Name	Common Name
EURO-ASIAN	
carnica	Carniolan
caucasica	Caucasian
cecropia	Macedonian
cypria	Cyprian
ligustica	Italian (yellow)
mellifera	German (dark)
remipes	Transcaucasian
syriaca	Syrian
AFRICAN	
adansonii	
capensis	
intermissa	
lamarckii	
litorea	
major	
monticola	
nubica	
sahariensis	
scutellata	

Behavior and characteristics of different races of bees have been studied over the years. Typical traits of interest to beekeepers usually are described in subjective terms and for an average colony. There is no one best race of bees; each beekeeper and each region has its own unique colony requirements. For example, overwintering ability is important if colonies are maintained in colder climates, especially if the individual is unable to move to a more temperate region in winter. Gentle bees are preferred, but if the colony is in an area where predators are abundant then it would not necessarily survive. There have been gradual population shifts of races in some areas. The German (dark) bees have been gradually replaced by Italians in the United States; Syrians by Italians in Israel; and Carniolans by Germans in northern and central Europe. In Brazil the Brazilian-African hybrid is replacing the Italians.

RACES

The German or dark bees originated in northern Europe, west of the Alps. They were the first race brought to the North American continent. This race was crossed with Caucasian, Carniolan, and Italian, and for practical purposes, the German race has been gradually replaced or lost. These bees have a tendency to be more defensive and readily sting.

The colony tends to increase in size slowly in the spring, but is reported to have good wintering ability which is a desirable trait. Other races, under favorable conditions, will increase their colony size rather dramatically; if the nectar flow suddenly stops, the colony starves. The German bee, on the other hand, builds up its colony size slowly—and less frequently exhausts its food supply. This bee is believed to have a short tongue and does poorly on certain clovers because it cannot reach the nectar.

The Italian bee is slightly smaller than the German bee, but has a longer tongue (½ mm longer). Queens were brought to the United States in the late 1850's. There are those who maintain that it is this race that made commercial beekeeping possible and profitable in the United States. This race is noted for its gentleness, although there are variations. The Italian bee tends to be prolific and noted to build large colonies quickly. If little nectar is available, the colonies tend to starve. Some beekeepers feel bees of this race have a strong tendency to rob or steal honey from other colonies. This is an undesirable trait since robbing also spreads disease.

The Carniolan bee originated from the southern part of Austria, Macedonia, and along the Danube River area. This bee is noted for its gentleness and it has very little inclination to rob honey from other colonies. They have a great tendency to swarm. Next to the Italians, the Carniolans are second in popularity on a worldwide basis.

Caucasians are noted for their liberal use of propolis within the hive. Propolis is a gum-like material collected from plants and used by bees to seal cracks and crevices in the hive. Heavily propolized hives are difficult to manipulate. Bees of the Caucasian race tend to drift from one hive to another, and are also prone to rob other colonies. As the name implies, these bees originated in the Caucasus of southern Russia.

SOCIAL ORGANIZATION

One unique characteristic of the honey bee is its highly developed social organization. The basic purpose of such a system is to increase efficiency through a division of labor and to extend life of the female. A colony functions like an individual; it gathers and consumes food, protects itself, grows, and reproduces. A highly developed colony like that of the honey bee does not die, although individual components die and are replaced.

Under catastrophic conditions, such as starvation, a colony will perish. The evolution of social insects can be easily observed in the different kinds of bees. The solitary bees, as the name implies, are insects which have little or nothing to do with one another except to mate. Some females will scatter their eggs. The developing larvae are then on their own. Some solitary bees go one step further. After mating, the female finds and builds her own nest. This could be a hollow stem of a plant, a nail hole or drilled hole 64 mm (about ¼ in. diameter) in a board, or any similar cavity. She collects pollen and nectar, forms it into a small pellet, and places it in the bottom of the hole. She then deposits an egg on this material. The pollen and nectar will serve as food for the developing larvae. The cell is sealed, then a second pellet and egg are placed directly above it. The process is repeated until the hole is completely filled. The top egg will hatch first (last in, first out). She continues to build or find nests and never sees her offspring.

Some of these solitary bees are very effective crop pollinators and efforts are made to provide artificial nesting sites for them. Successful nesting sites have been made from soda straws or boards with 48 mm (³/₁₆ in.) drilled holes. These nesting sites are then placed near crops, such as alfalfa, which require or benefit from this insect pollinator.

The earliest or most primitive form of social life can be observed in some Halidae bees. The female lives long enough to see the eggs hatch, and she provides the developing larvae with some pollen and nectar when needed, rather than providing them with all the food before hatching. Such feeding behavior is called progressive provisioning. When all the food required for complete development is provided at one time, it is referred to as massive provisioning.

The next higher level of socialization is when the female starts a new nest of her own each spring. She provides food for larvae, and lives long enough so some of her offspring (all female and slightly smaller) continue to live with her and help collect food for other larvae and build additional cells. These workers do not mate. Later males and larger females are reared, and after mating, the young females hibernate either alone or in groups until the following spring when they start the next generation. The old queen, workers, and males die in the fall. A new nest is constructed each year.

The next higher stage in socialization is seen in the bumblebee. A nest is started each spring by an overwintered fertilized queen. Initially, she is capable of doing everything—build the nest, forage, lay eggs, and feed larvae. The first offspring are incomplete or imperfect females not capable of mating. These workers assume foraging duties and the queen continues to lay eggs. As food becomes more plentiful and the colony larger in numbers, queens and males are raised. Mating occurs between members of different colonies. Here is noted a well-marked differentiation between the queen and worker caste, but the queen can and must carry out all duties that are later performed by the workers. Each fall the entire colony dies except for the fertilized queens.

The next higher stage is in the Meliponid bees. These bees had been kept for honey production at one time in South America. Caste differentiation is well marked. The queen cannot collect pollen, and the colony is perennial. Swarming occurs from time to time, and the larvae are fed by mass provisioning of the cells rather than progressive feeding.

The highest degree of socialization is found in the honey bee. Colonies have a well-developed caste system, and the queen differs in many ways from workers. The queen, essentially an egg-laying machine, has lost the ability to build a nest, forage for food, and feed larvae. Larvae are fed progressively.

A well-structured social organization is also found in ants (Hymenoptera) and termites (Isoptera). It is generally believed that their social structure evolved earlier than that of bees and wasps. This is based on the fact that there are no solitary members in these groups, and there is also a well-defined caste system.

That the honey bee attracted man's attention years ago is not unusual. This bee produces a sweet, wholesome food, honey, and a useful product, beeswax. It also has an interesting and highly organized social organization within the colony. The fact that the honey bee possesses a formidable defensive weapon—the stinger—offers challenge to others.

BIBLIOGRAPHY

BORROR, D.J., D.M. DELONG, and C.A. TRIPLEHORN. 1976. Introduction to the Study of Insects. 4th edition. Holt, Rinehart, and Winston, New York.

RICHARDS, O.W., and R.G. DAVIS. 1977. Imms' General Textbook of Entomology. 10th edition. John Wiley & Sons, New York.

2

Development of an Industry

Because of insects' size, their fossil records are not as abundant and complete as they are for other animals. The earliest evidence of primitive insects is found in the Paleozoic era approximately 400 million years ago in the Devonian period. The honey bee is a more recent arrival, evolving during the Jurassic period in the Mesozoic era 180 million years ago, about the same time flowering plants and birds made their appearance. Additional information on phylogenetic relationships and evolution can be found in Ross (1964).

The ancestors of the honey bee undoubtedly were wasps or a similar type of creature which, like some common wasps today, builds nests in sheltered locations. *Apis florea* and *Apis dorsata* are examples of primitive bees which build a single exposed comb. As climatic changes took place or this primitive creature dispersed to more hostile regions, those colonies which built nests in cavities had an adaptive advantage. Wasps today are either scavengers or carnivores—so too was the primitive bee or its immediate ancestor. While "meat" may provide a better diet when conditions are favorable and food plentiful, those creatures which were able to adapt to a vegetarian diet, gather and store food for periods when none was available, had a definite advantage. Another possible explanation is the appearance of flowering plants, which provided a new source of food—pollen and nectar. Bees were able to move in and take advantage of this new situation. Because of this adaptation, bees were able to spread to practically all parts of Europe, Asia, and Africa, except in the desert and high mountainous regions where the required vegetation was not available.

Primitive people interested in honey were not beekeepers, but honey hunters. The earliest hives were hollow trees in forested areas. In cultural centers in the Middle East where forests were lacking, small caves in hillsides probably served as natural hives.

Etchings on cave walls in Spain, dated around 7000 B.C., could be interpreted as depicting a person using smoke to rob a colony of bees of

9

its honey. Paintings inside tombs, dating back to 3000 B.C., provide evidence that Egyptians were interested in bees. Aristotle in 334 B.C. recorded observations on bees in his treatise, *Natural Science*, in which he recognized the different races of bees. His writings suggest that he had a type of hive with an opening that allowed him to observe the activities within, or made some type of movable comb, suspended in a box-like hive. In 40 B.C., Virgil described how to make a hive of cork and suggested it be located in the shade and protected from animals. Through the centuries, many others wrote on the subject, often combining imagination with observations.

Early Apiculturists observed that a swarm of bees would take up residence in any suitable cavity. To help bees, or to keep them near home, hollowed-out logs were provided. In the Middle East, people noted that bees would establish a colony in pottery vessels used for storing grain and water. This type of hive is still used today in some of those less developed areas. Baskets woven with coils of straw appeared a little later, and is probably the origin of the skep which is still used in a few parts of Europe today. These primitive hives performed the necessary functions of sheltering the colony from wind, rain, and hot weather like the modern hive today. Primitive hives were small because they had to be handled as one unit. To obtain honey, the bees had to be killed by plunging the entire unit into hot water or smoking it with burning sulfur. The small hive encouraged swarming—which was the way colony numbers were increased. Swarming was not understood, and most operational decisions were made on a hit or miss basis. Sometimes luck was good, other times not so good. Bees were valuable since they provided honey, which was not only a food and sweetening agent, but a very important medicine purported to cure many ailments. By not understanding the biology and behavior of bees, many different kinds of folklore stories developed—some very interesting, others amusing, and a few not too far off, based on our understanding today.

FOLKLORE

Spontaneous generation was accepted as fact for many years, and bees were thought to have arisen from bodies of dead cattle. Undoubtedly the rib cage made a good home for a swarm, especially if the skeleton was still covered with the hide. The same belief was held in Africa, but with a lion acting as host. According to German folklore, bees were put on this world to make wax for church candles. In Egyptian mythology, bees originated from the sun god Ra. The bee was the symbol of Hindu gods Indra, Krishna, and Vishnu. Through the ages and up to today, bee stings have been regarded as having medicinal value, especially for rheumatism, arthritis, and neuritis.

In some parts of Europe, bees were thought to be messengers of God and closely associated with death and dying. If a member of the household died, bees were to be informed; otherwise they would swarm, die, or stop making honey. The Irish tell their secrets to bees and also inform them of new projects. If this is done, bees will prosper. Bees won't prosper if they are argued over or bought on Friday. In fact, the first swarm should not be bought but bartered. It is bad luck to have a swarm come to you, even in a dream. To dream of bees in a swarm is an omen of death, and to dream of a sting means a friend will betray you. If you dream of bees producing honey, you are in for some money. If a bee comes into your house, this means a stranger is coming. If it flies in— then out, this is good luck; but if it dies inside—bad luck. If you hold a bee in your hand, it won't sting you while you hold your breath.

As claimed in Irish, Japanese, and Jewish legend, bees were to have routed invaders and saved the homeland. The world atlas lists ten communities whose names are bee-related, such as Bee, Beetown, and Bee Ridge. Thus, bees have been closely associated with civilization.

BEGINNINGS OF AN INDUSTRY

Up to the 16th Century, the beekeeper's operation was simple. Swarms were captured in late spring or early summer, and in fall the combs were cut out—wax and honey separated—and those colonies kept over winter were fed additional honey. Their relationship to pollination was unknown. The queen was thought to be a king bee. Sex of workers and drones was unknown, and so was the fact that wax was secreted by the workers.

Dramatic changes in beekeeping began to take place at the beginning of the 16th Century. About this time science, though primitive, began to influence civilization. Fundamental observations on the life cycle and biology of the honey bee and other organisms were underway. In 1586, the beekeeping world was told that the large bee everyone called a king bee was actually a female and therefore should be called a queen. In 1609 and 1637, respectively, drones were described as males and workers as females. Primary facts on mating were not discovered until 1771. Bees were an integral part of many European monasteries, and when they were destroyed by the Reformation, beekeeping was dealt a severe blow.

The industrial revolution in Europe brought people to the cities, which also meant changes in agriculture. Some self-sufficient farms or small villages started developing into commercial enterprises. Beekeeping also began to change. Those people with an interest, knowledge and ingenuity to manage bees enlarged their operation and sold honey. The conventional hive was a crudely constructed box, or the typical woven inverted basket-like skep. Then, as now, progressive individuals were interested in improving the efficiency of their operation. One innovation was to add an extension to the top of the skep, somewhat resembling a special cap. Bees would build combs in it and if nectar was available, fill it with honey; but the queen would not lay eggs in it. This is probably the origin of the honey super, a term still used today. The boxes used as hives had doors on top, or in back, through which combs of honey could be removed. Perhaps equipment was not standardized or uniform because no design proved completely satisfactory. Some hives had bars across the top of the box on which bees suspended combs. These bars and attached combs could be lifted out or pulled through the back door. In all cases, combs were broken or destroyed because bees would attach them to the walls of the hive. Some beekeepers had impressive operations even when compared to our standards today. A Ukrainian, Peter Prokopovich, was reported to have up to 10,000 colonies. He used movable combs and had vertical compartments. The top bars in the lower compartment had notches large enough to allow bees free passage from one compartment to the other. This was the first clue to what was to become a fundamental discovery in beehive engineering.

MIGRATION TO THE NEW WORLD

Europeans began establishing permanent colonies in the new world in the late 16th and 17th Centuries. They took with them only items of importance such as cows, horses, and of course bees. The date on which the first colony of bees arrived in North America is not recorded but is believed to be sometime around 1620. Inventory records in Virginia list beeswax in 1622 and actually colony records start in 1638. The new continent proved to be well suited for the honey bee. Maple, basswood, oak, willow, and aspen are examples of trees which produced nectar and pollen; so did shrubs such as hazelnut, sumac, blackberries, and raspberries; and such flowers as golden rod and asters. Bees do well at the edge of the forest. Clearing trees for farming provided an ideal environment for them. Honey bees, then as now, sometimes swarmed and got away. Hollow trees provided excellent natural hives and bees spread westward. While the Appalachian mountains provided a natural barrier, it is believed that bees were able to spread westward by four principal routes: through the Cumberland Gap, up the Mohawk River Valley, along the Ohio River Valley, and south along the Gulf Coast. Undoubtedly, the early settlers also took bees with them as they moved westward. Natural swarming and natural migration alone cannot account for their rapid movement westward. They arrived in the vicinity of Ohio in 1754,

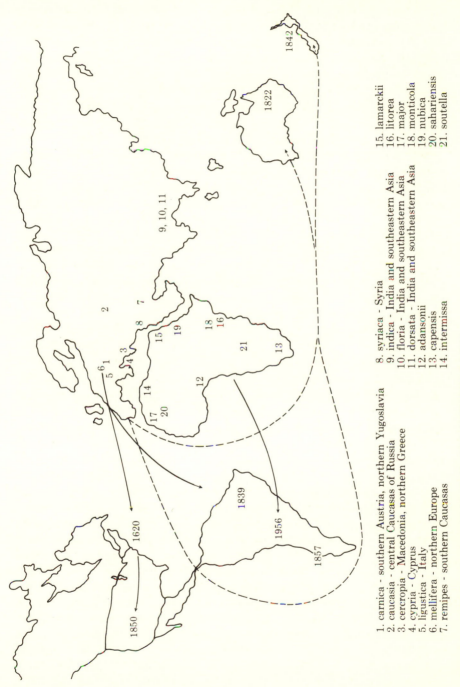

FIG. 2.1. DISTRIBUTION AND MIGRATION OF HONEY BEE RACES

1. carnica - southern Austria, northern Yugoslavia
2. caucasia - central Caucasas of Russia
3. cercropia - Macedonia, northern Greece
4. cypria - Cyprus
5. ligustica - Italy
6. mellifera - northern Europe
7. remipes - southern Caucasas
8. syriaca - Syria
9. indica - India and southeastern Asia
10. floria - India and southeastern Asia
11. dorsata - India and southeastern Asia
12. adansonii
13. capensis
14. intermissa
15. lamarckii
16. litorea
17. major
18. monticola
19. nubica
20. sahariensis
21. soutella

Tennessee in 1750, and as far west as eastern Texas, eastern Nebraska, and Minnesota by 1820. Whether they first arrived on the west coast by ship or overland by covered wagon is unknown, but they were there by 1850. Indians referred to bees as white man's flies and viewed them with mixed feelings.

Bees arrived in Australia by 1822, South America in 1839, and in New Zealand in 1842. By then they were on all major land masses of the world.

The honey bee adapted well to its new environment. In fact, it does better in terms of honey production per colony today in the new world than in its original European home.

A NEW ERA

A new era in beekeeping began in 1851. A common problem facing beekeepers was the fact that bees firmly attached the comb to the sides and top of the hive and there was no way to remove the honey without breaking the comb. Innovative beekeepers built frames and bars which they hoped would be used by bees so combs could be easily removed. Their efforts were without success until a minister and hobby beekeeper discovered one simple fact. Rev. Lorenzo L. Langstroth noted that if he allowed between 80 and 95 mm ($5/16$ ft and $3/8$ in.) space between component parts of the hive—just enough so bees could crawl through—they would not fill in the area with wax or propolis. Spaces less than 64 mm ($1/4$ in.) were sealed, and in spaces greater than 95 mm ($3/8$ in.), bees built wax comb. Langstroth immediately recognized the significance of this observation and patented the phenomenon of *bee space*. Equipment manufacturers now consider these facts in designing equipment.

A biography of Rev. L.L. Langstroth by Naile was recently reprinted. It vividly describes his interest in bees, his efforts to promote the revolutionary hive, and his efforts to protect his patent.

The basic concept of the Langstroth hive was quickly adapted in the United States and Europe by progressive beekeepers. This led to other inventions: the beeswax foundation in 1857 by Johannes Mehring, a German, and the extractor in 1865 by Major Hrushka, an Austrian. Under the influence of the industrial revolution, enterprising individuals further developed these ideas. In the United States, A.I. Root produced a roller press that made wax foundation commercially, and L.L. Langstroth, C. Dadant, and M. Quinby modified the extractor to suit the needs of the commercial beekeeper. These inventions completed the evolution of beekeeping equipment and made possible the growth of beekeeping from a gardening or small farming sideline to a full-scale commercial enterprise.

It was during the Civil War period that Congress made two historic decisions. It created the U.S. Department of Agriculture as an agency of the federal government and passed the Morrill Act which established the Land Grant Universities. Benefits and ramifications of these two decisions are beyond the scope of this book, but they also affected bees and beekeeping. The U.S. Department of Agriculture began researching problems associated with bees, beekeeping, and honey production in 1885, and many Land Grant Institutions recognized beekeeping (Apiculture) as an academic subject worthy of teaching and research. These efforts continue today. There are currently six U.S. Department of Agriculture Field Laboratories involved in research on problems associated with bees. Many are operated in conjunction with universities, and each has a primary mission such as investigations into bee disease and colony management. Some of the secondary missions are associated with local or regional concerns. Through the Science and Education Administration-Extension, in cooperation with the states, continuing education programs are conducted also. Currently, 26 states have professional personnel who devote at least part of their time to apicultural education.

The evolution of the beekeeping industry has been long and gradual. During this time man has developed suitable equipment so that colonies can be efficiently managed, selected some desirable genetic lines, and gained some insights into their behavior. Bees have defied domestication and basic equipment has changed little since 1851. Substitutes are now available for honey and beeswax, but not for pollination. So the future for *Apis mellifera* appears bright and challenging for man.

BIBLIOGRAPHY

MORE, D. 1976. The History and Natural History of the Honey Bee. Universe Books, New York.

NAILE, F. 1976. America's Master Bee Culture. The Life of L.L. Langstroth. Cornell University Press, Ithaca, N.Y.

ROSS, H.H. 1964. Textbook of Entomology. 3rd edition. John Wiley & Sons, New York.

3

Structure of Honey Bee

The queen honey bee is easily distinguished from workers and drones by size and shape. Her wings are shorter in proportion to body length than those of workers or drones, and the abdomen is distinctly pointed. A laying queen is much longer than a drone and a little broader than a worker. Drones are larger and stouter than either queens or workers, and workers are the smallest, but most numerous, members of a colony. Each develops in its own type of cell. The queen develops in a specially constructed vertically hanging cell, and drones in large horizontal ones, 287.1 cells per deci^2 (16.5 per in.^{2}). Worker cells are smallest, 478.5 cells per deci^2 (27.5 per in.^{2}). Cell counts are based on one side of the comb.

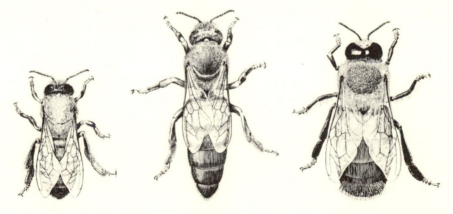

From USDA

FIG. 3.1. WORKER, QUEEN, AND DRONE OF THE HONEY BEE *APIS MELLIFERA*

Some knowledge of honey bee anatomy is helpful to understand and appreciate their capability and behavior. Differences among queen,

17

drone, and worker will be mentioned where they exist.

The honey bee resembles the typical generalized insect. In the adult form its body is divided into three parts—head, thorax, and abdomen. It also has two pairs of wings, six legs, an open circulatory system, a dorsal brain, and a ventral nerve cord.

Through natural selection and evolution, the honey bee has developed into an efficient, highly specialized creature. Very conspicuous and unique to bees are body hairs because they have short side branches. While their functions are not completely understood, they are connected to nerves, undoubtedly serving as mechanical or tactile receptors, since the exoskeleton is rather insensitive to touch. Some hairs serve as organs of balance so that the bees are able to know their position in relation to gravity. Old workers often lose many of their hairs, but whether this affects their performance is unknown.

Like many insects, bees have large compound eyes. Each is composed of hundreds of small visual units called ommatidia with their own lens and light-sensitive tissues. Vision through a compound eye produces a mosaic. The ommatidium directly in line with the object is clearly seen, but those on the edge less distinctly. It is supposed that the bee sees as many points of light as there are ommatidia, and any slight movement is detected instantly because of changing light patterns. Such eyes are thought to be able to judge close distance very accurately. Their eyes are sensitive to polarized light and to yellow, blue-green, blue-violet, and ultraviolet. They cannot see red; it is thought that red and black would appear as varying shades of gray.

Eyes of drones are much larger in proportion to the head than those of a queen or worker. Bees also have three ocelli. Although their function is not fully understood, it is believed that they are sensitive to changes in light intensity which affects behavior and activities. Additional details related to the structure of compound eye and insect vision can be found in the book by Horridge (1975).

Antennae are important sensory organs which are covered with minute sensory receptacles. While it is difficult to determine the exact function of each type or variety, undoubtedly these receptacles respond to such common stimuli as odor, pheromones, and touch, and possibly others. Antennae on a drone have one additional segment.

The mandibles, like those of the typical insect with chewing mouth parts, are attached to the sides of the oral opening and move sideways. Those of the drone are smaller and differ slightly in shape from those of a queen and worker. Worker mandibles are used for gnawing pollen out of the cells, for manipulating wax to build and replace comb, and as a grasping instrument for general housekeeping chores, such as removing debris from the colony. Attached to each mandible is a large gland, the mandibular gland, which is located in the head. In the queen this gland

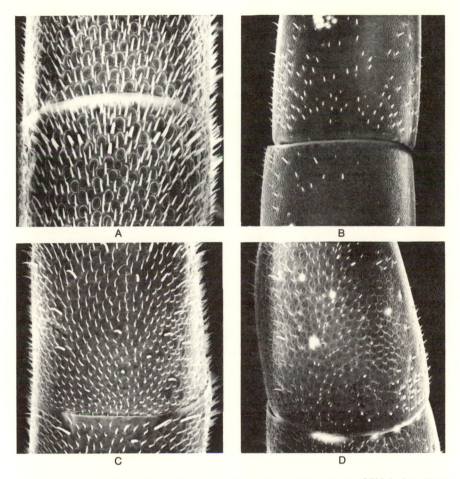

FIG. 3.2. DIFFERENCES IN NUMBERS, KINDS AND DISTRIBUTION OF SENSORY RECEPTORS ON ANTENNAE OF: (A) DORSAL SURFACE—WORKER (330X); (B) DORSAL SURFACE—DRONE (220X); (C) VENTRAL SURFACE—WORKER (330X); (D) VENTRAL SURFACE—DRONE (220X)

secretes a chemical called Queen substance, a powerful sex-attractant, and in workers it is believed that the secretion is used to soften wax during comb construction.

Bees are rather unique in that they have both chewing and sucking mouth parts. The proboscis is a retractable tube through which they can ingest nectar and water. When not in use, it retracts automatically by curving backwards. Between the mouth and the esophagus is a sucking pump, a large muscled wall sac within the head. It serves as an organ of egestion and ingestion inasmuch as regurgitation of nectar and honey is

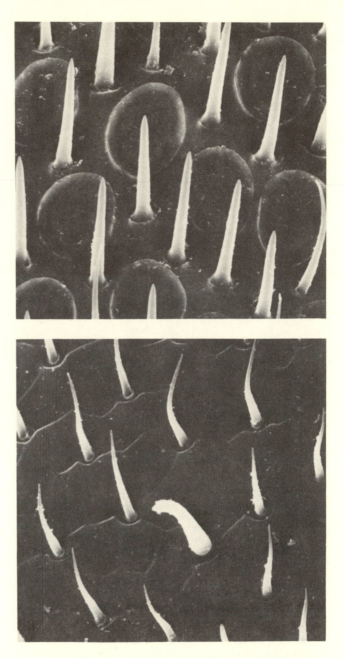

Courtesy of University of Wisconsin Entomology
Department–SEM–Laboratory

FIG. 3.3. SENSORY ORGANS ON ANTENNAE (2200X)
(Upper) Dorsal surface. (Lower) Ventral surface.

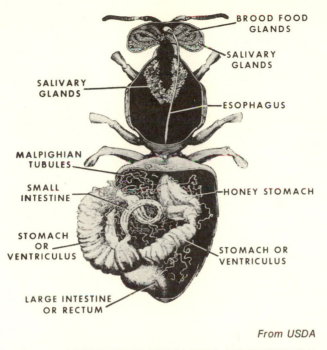

From USDA

FIG. 3.4. ALIMENTARY TRACT, GLANDS, AND EXCRETORY
SYSTEM OF A WORKER HONEY BEE

as important to the colony as is withdrawing nectar from flowers. Also within the head are salivary and brood food glands.

The alimentary canal begins at the mouth and leads to the sucking pump, which goes to the esophagus, and then to the honey stomach. The honey stomach (crop) is capable of expansion. Immediately beyond is the proventriculus, which works like a mouth to the stomach. For example, it allows pollen to pass to the stomach (ventriculus) but retains nectar. Likewise, it prevents contents from the stomach to be regurgitated back to the crop. Leading from the stomach is the looped and coiled intestine and finally the rectum. The rectum is capable of great distention when bees are confined for prolonged periods during cold winter months when cleansing flights are not possible.

The malpighian tubules serve as the excretory system. These are small coiled tubes which float in the body cavity, and absorb wastes—primarily uric acid and salts—and transport them to the intestine. They join the intestine at the junction of the intestine and stomach.

In many respects, the honey bee is no different than other multicellular organisms. Its cells require oxygen and a means of eliminating carbon dioxide. This is accomplished by a respiratory system which consists of trachea and spiracles because its exoskeleton is not designed for breathing as is the integument of some other animals. Trachea are hollow branching tubes with rigid, spiral thickened walls which lead from an opening in the body wall, the spiracle, to all parts of the body. Three spiracles are located on the thorax, and six on the abdomen. Oxygen is transported directly to the cells by these tubes, and carbon dioxide is eliminated in a similar manner. Respiration (like our breathing) can be partly affected by bodily contractions because of the rigid tubules.

The honey bee has rather unique heat requirements. Body temperature is maintained within relatively narrow limits compared to other cold-blooded animals. Honey bees cluster to retain metabolic heat, and fan to cool when the temperature is too high. In flight, excess heat is produced and must be eliminated. Thermo regulation in bumble bees is summarized by Heinrich (1977). Undoubtedly, many of the same principles described would also apply to honey bees.

All insects have an open circulatory system. Blood does not flow in vessels but throughout the body cavity. It is circulated by a long pulsating tube, along the dorsal side, from the head to abdomen. The portion located in the abdomen is called the heart, and in the thorax, the aorta. Blood is pumped forward and out the sides through little slits called ostia. Basically this system is not a very efficient mechanism compared to the mammalian circulatory system; however, insect blood carries only nutrients, not carbon dioxide and oxygen. Because of its open circulatory system any major wound, such as losing a stinger, is fatal to the honey bee because it quickly bleeds to death.

Animals have the ability to respond and adjust to changing conditions in the environment. Specialized cells or groups of cells that detect these changes are sense organs, and cells which transmit impulses are nerves. Like other higher animals, the honey bee has well developed sensory, motor, and association nerve fibers. The central nervous system is quite similar to that of other insects. The brain is located dorsally in the head and the nerve cord along the ventral side of the thorax and abdomen. Impulses detected by the head, eyes, and antennae are transmitted to the brain and nerve cord. Those impulses direct many natural activities. But if the head is removed it still can perform functions controlled by the nerve cord, such as walking, flying, and even stinging.

Bees have no known auditory organs, but it can be easily demonstrated that they respond to vibrations. Whether these are detected by the legs, antennae, hairs, or a combination of them is unknown. Certain frequencies will make bees freeze. Experienced beekeepers can hear one or two "angry" or highly irritated bees when working a colony. Undoubtedly, this sound is produced by wing beat, and such behavior rarely stimulates others to be more defensive. This further points out that they probably do not hear sound as we know it.

The abdomen houses the principal visceral organs such as stomach and intestine, as well as the reproductive system and its associated structures. Workers have some specialized glands. The larval honey bee has ten abdominal segments. During metamorphosis, the first abdominal segment is fused into the thorax. Segments 8, 9, and 10 are greatly modified and concealed within segment 7. The adult bee then appears to have only six segments. It is customary to number the segments in the adult so that they correspond to the larval segment numbers. Four pairs of wax-secreting glands are on the ventral surface of segments 4 through 7. Under proper conditions, specific cells undergo modification and become glandular, capable of secreting wax. The opening is covered by the overlapping plate so it appears that wax exudes from between segments. After the wax-secreting period is completed, the glandular cells degenerate. Nassanoff's gland is located on the dorsal surface of segment 7. It secretes several important chemicals. They are geraniol, citral, nerolic, and geranic acids, and other unidentified materials. When emitting odor from this gland, the abdomen is flexed in such a manner that the surface of the gland is exposed, thus releasing chemicals into the air stream.

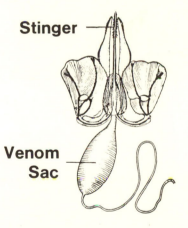

Stinger

Venom Sac

FIG. 3.5. DIAGRAMMATIC SKETCH OF THE STINGER AND ASSOCIATED STRUCTURES

The stinger on the honey bee is similar to the ovipositor on other Hymenopterous insects which insert eggs into the body of their host insect or into woody tissue of plants. It has been slightly modified to inject venom instead of eggs. Although the stinger appears to be one structure, it is composed of three separate pieces. One piece has three recurved teeth, and the other two have nine or ten. When not in use, it is retracted into the sting chamber. When stinging, the worker flexes her abdomen abruptly downward and with a sudden jab inserts the stinger into the skin of its victim. Muscles now begin working alternately, forcing parts of the stinger deeper into the wound, even if the apparatus is ripped off the body. Venom produced in the poison gland and stored in the poison sac or reservoir is injected. The stinger of a queen is longer, more curved, and more firmly attached to the body. Its barbs are somewhat smaller, but the poison gland is larger. Although the queen is reluctant to sting, she can and will, and people stung by a queen say that the sting is more painful than one from a worker.

Reproductive systems are fully developed only in drones and queens; they are present but undeveloped in workers. Testes are a pair of small flat bodies inside the abdomen, attached to the vas deferens, which leads to a long slender sac called the seminal vesicle. The seminal vesicle opens into the lower end of the mucous gland, and it in turn empties into one ejaculatory duct, which leads to the penis, from which spermatozoa are discharged at mating.

The ovaries are large, pear-shaped structures composed of closely-packed tubules, ovarioles. Each is attached to an oviduct which unites into a short, common oviduct, which leads to the vagina. The vagina opens to the body wall at the base of the stinger.

Dorsal to the vagina is a spherical structure, the spermatheca, in which sperm received during mating is stored. As eggs pass down the oviduct, they mature and sperm is released from the spermatheca, which fertilizes the egg in the vagina. Fertilization is a voluntary action by the queen. Fertilized eggs will develop into workers or queens, and those that are unfertilized become drones.

Wings of honey bees are adapted for agile maneuverability, rapid flight, and strength for carrying a heavy load. Each is hinged by its base and free to move up and down, forward and backward, and can undergo a twisting and partial rotation. In flight they are united. A fold on the front wing is designed to receive a hook (hamuli) on the second, so the two wings on each side function as one unit. All wing movements are controlled by a complex system of muscles in the thorax. They are not attached to wings themselves, but to movable structures of the thorax. Considering the simplicity of the mechanism, the efficiency of bee flight is remarkable. Even without a steering device, they can hover, fly forward, backwards, sideways, and turn with remarkable ease.

Honey bee legs are divided into six principal parts or segments attached to each other by flexible joints. The segment nearest the thorax is the coxa, followed by trochanter, femur, tibia, tarsus, and pretarsus. The last segment is further subdivided into five parts—the basi-tarsis is the largest and sometimes called the planta. While the joints are flexible, they can move only in one plane. However, each leg has a number of joints that move at different planes which offsets this disadvantage, so

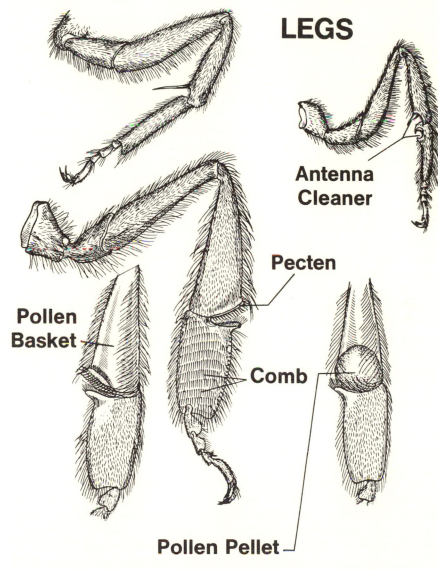

LEGS

Antenna Cleaner

Pecten

Pollen Basket

Comb

Pollen Pellet

FIG. 3.6. LEGS OF WORKER HONEY BEE WITH SPECIALIZED STRUCTURES

the legs are a rather versatile structure.

In addition to being organs of locomotion, legs of honey bees are specially modified to collect pollen. The inner margin of the first pair is equipped with a deep notch, the antennal cleaner. The margin is fringed with a comb-like row of small spines. When the antenna becomes covered with pollen, the worker merely pulls it through this notch for cleaning. Antennal cleaners are found also on drones and queens. Brushes are on the inner surface of the basi-tarsis of the first two pair of legs. With the first pair she is able to remove pollen and debris from her head, eyes, and mouth parts, while her second pair are used to clean the thorax. The tibia of the third pair of legs on workers has a pollen basket formed by its concave shape and the spines along the outer edge. By a series of manipulations and movements, she is able to transfer pollen collected in the brushes to the pollen basket. Pollen moistened with nectar is packed into the form of a pellet. Upon returning to the hive, she locates a suitable cell, examines it with her head and antennae, turns around, backs in, and dislodges the pellet. Spines on her legs help her dislodge the pellet from the pollen basket. Additional details on the anatomy of the honey bee can be found in Snodgrass (1956).

So each individual is able to contribute its share to the success of the colony, the honey bee evolved its own unique structures. The manner in which they perform vital functions will be the subject of the next chapter.

BIBLIOGRAPHY

HEINRICH, B. 1977. The physiology of exercise in the bumblebee. Am. Sci. *65,* 455-465.

HORRIDGE, G.A. 1975. The Compound Eye and Vision of Insects. Claredon Press, Oxford.

SNODGRASS, R.E. 1956. Anatomy of the Honey Bee. Cornell University Press, Ithaca, N.Y.

4

Components of the Colony

There has always been considerable interest in watching the activities and behavior of honey bees. As more is learned about their true nature, our ideas and understanding of what is happening change. Early observers interpreted activities and behavior in terms of human values and experiences. They used terms such as "become angry" or act in an "uncivilized manner" to describe colony defense. Comb construction was termed clever, ingenious, or smart.

Honey bees have sensory organs and a nervous system, and they respond to light, odor, vibrations, touch, taste, gravity, and possibly electrical and magnetic forces. The exact mechanism by which these stimuli are processed by the nervous system is unknown. It is doubtful that they make decisions—more than likely they are programmed robots designed to survive. Honey bees are also governed by genetics and such factors as pheromones, circadian rhythm, photoperiod, temperature, and crowding. To help understand behavior, it is convenient to treat components of the colony individually realizing that no one organism exists in a vacuum.

QUEEN

The queen was recognized in the colony by early beekeepers long before her function was known. Early writers described her as the sultan, Rex, or King bee, because they knew that if she was missing the colony did not function properly. However, Aristotle hinted that she was the mother of the bees and ruled over workers. In 1609 Rev. Charles Butler in France announced to the world that what everyone called the King bee was actually a female and should be called a Queen. He suspected that all workers were females and that they mated with drones, then laid eggs. Some 130 years later, the thought prevailed that the queen laid eggs, but drones fertilized them in the cells. It was in 1771 that the Royal Beekeeper for Empress Maria Theresa in Vienna, Anton Janscha, described how the newly emerged queen left the hive and returned mated.

When the queen honey bee completes her development, she chews her way out of the cell with her mandibles. The cell cap is cut almost all the way around, and she is able to push the lid to one side and crawl out. Many times the lid will remain attached to the old queen cell for several days. On emerging, she eats some honey and begins to wander within the colony. Within a short time she searches out potential rivals and kills them. However, if a queen is produced under swarm conditions and the old queen has not left, workers will feed the emerging queen before she crawls out. This feeding apparently slows her emergence from an hour to several days. If a second or even a third queen is in this same colony, they will likewise feed them. When conditions are suitable for swarming, the old queen and some workers leave to establish a new home. The other queens placed in "holding" will also leave—producing what beekeepers call secondary and tertiary swarms.

When the old queen is replaced without swarming (supercedure), the newly emerged queen ignores her mother; but if she meets another, they will fight until one is killed. She will now seek out sealed queen cells and kill the occupant. It is not unusual to have a mother-daughter combination living harmoniously in one colony. In reviewing the literature on behavior of the newly emerged queen, it is quite obvious that there is considerable variation among individuals of different colonies.

When several newly emerged queens are free on the comb and/or ready to emerge, they can produce an audible shrill sound called "piping." Sound is produced by vibrations of small plates on the thorax amplified by contact with the substrate. At this stage, they will also respond to artificial sounds from 600 to 2,000 cycles per second. Workers in the immediate vicinity "freeze" or stop what they are doing for several seconds. There is no clear explanation as to the function or value of this behavior. Some writers believe that one queen is challenging her rivals and others are answering in defiance.

Most matings take place between the sixth and tenth day after emergence, although it could range between the third and eleventh day. Before taking her mating flight, the queen will take several exploratory flights which may last 2-30 minutes. The mating flight or flights may last from 5-20 minutes. Most mating flights occur between 2 PM and 4 PM on days when the temperature is above 20°C (68°F). This phenomenon poses problems for commercial queen producers who rely on natural matings. If the weather is unfavorable for mating during this critical period, queens do not receive sufficient sperm or may not even be mated. During mating, she acquires a lifetime supply of sperm which is maintained in her spermatheca like part of her own body tissue. While many beekeepers routinely replace queens after one, two, or three years, some are known to live seven or eight years. Specific details on honey bee matings have been reported by Gary (1963) and and Gary and Marston (1971).

Egg laying may begin as soon as 14 hours after she returns, but most start in 2 to 3 days and will continue the rest of her life, except for periods during late fall and during shortage of pollen. Before mating, the queen appears to be somewhat ignored by workers in the colony. However, as soon as she is mated and begins to lay, a group of young bees form a crude circle around her, and constantly examine her with antennae, and groom or lick her with the proboscis. They constantly feed and remove excrement and any eggs that may have been accidently dropped. When she finds a cell which meets her requirements, she inserts her abdomen into it and deposits an egg.

Since the egg case is moist, it adheres firmly to the base of the cell. It is not unusual for some queens to occasionally place two eggs in one cell. This frequently occurs when a healthy laying queen is removed from a full-sized colony and placed with a small population of bees.

The queen honey bee is unique in that she "at pleasure" can control the sex of her offspring. It was in 1845 that Johann Dzierzon first proposed that drones are produced from unfertilized eggs, and queens and workers from fertilized ones. That eggs develop without fertilization (parthenogenesis) is not unique among insects. Some aphids and lice also develop in this manner.

Controlled sex is not a simple phenomenon. Normally, drone eggs are laid in larger cells or what is referred to as drone comb. Before depositing an egg, the queen examines it with her head, antennae, and front legs. There is some evidence to suggest that the front legs are used as a caliper to measure cell size, and then she determines whether to lay an unfertilized egg or one that is fertilized. She can apparently switch from fertilized to non-fertilized quite rapidly. An unanswered question is how does she free her vagina from stray sperm so eggs are not accidently fertilized.

Before the queen can lay a drone egg, a suitable cell must be available. In spring when pollen is abundant, workers appear to cooperate by constructing drone cells in every "conceivable" space, and she readily uses them. Drones are not produced even though cells are available when pollen is in short supply, in late fall, and in very small colonies.

The queen appears to move in a deliberate and purposeful manner. Cells containing eggs are frequently crossed and recrossed, but egg laying is confined to an ever expanding sphere. One criterion used to evaluate a good queen is the brood pattern. Eggs and larvae should be in a compact pattern, leaving few vacant cells.

In addition to being an egg-laying machine, the queen is also a chemical factory. The material or materials she produces keep the colony together as one organized unit. It takes very little practical experience working with bees before a person can tell whether the queen is present. It was C.G. Butler (1954) in England who used the term "queen substance" to describe some unidentified material which could be extracted from the body of a queen with ethyl alcohol that prevented the queenless colony of workers from raising their own queen, and it also suppressed ovary development in workers isolated from a normal colony. The substance has now been identified as a product of the mandibular gland and is 9-oxodecenoic acid and 9-hydroxydecenoic acid. This substance becomes spread over the queen and is carried throughout the colony during feeding. The chemical is not very stable since within one-half hour after a queen is removed, workers know it, as judged by their behavior.

DRONES

Drones are larger and stouter than queens or workers. Being specialists designed only for mating, they have no pollen basket, stinger, or wax glands. Their proboscis is shorter than that found on workers, and their eyes are much larger. When inside the colony, they stay near the brood area where workers between 2 and 26 days old feed them regurgitated nectar from their crop. First flights are taken in the afternoons between the fourth to fourteenth day, depending on the weather. Orientation flights are of relatively short duration, between 6 and 15 minutes, whereas a mating flight may be between 30 and 60 minutes. In flight, drones sound distinctly different from workers; apparently their wing beat is of a different frequency. Mating flights occur after they are 12 days old. Prior to these flights, they engorge on honey and thoroughly clean their antennae and eyes. They orientate on landmarks rather than use the sun as a compass to find their "drone congregation" sites. There is some evidence to suggest that drones mark out specific areas by pheromones. Whether this area attracts queens is unknown; however, queens mate with drones from colonies as far as ten miles away. The average drone will take about 25 flights in his lifetime over a period of 21 days, and 96% will return to the colony. A successful mating is fatal to the drone because the genitals are torn from the body, and, like the worker who loses its stinger, it bleeds to death. Only a small percentage are able to fulfill their natural function since 96% return to the hive.

WORKERS

Workers are the smallest, yet most numerous, members of the honey bee colony. They are underdeveloped females with small ovaries and are not capable of producing eggs under normal conditions. So well is communism developed that none act as individuals, and so well programmed is their behavior that they require no administrator or dictator. Practically all activities within the hive involve workers. These activities will be discussed in detail in the following chapter.

BIBLIOGRAPHY

BUTLER, C.G. 1954. The method and importance of the recognition by a colony of honey bees *(A. Mellifera)* of the presence of its queen. Trans. R. Entomol. Soc. London 105:11.

GARY, N.E. 1963. Observations of mating behavior in the honey bee. J. Apic. Res. *2* (1) 3-13.

GARY, N.E., and J. MARSTON. 1971. Mating behavior of drone honey bees with queen models *(Apis mellifera L.)*. Anim. Behav. *19*, 299-304.

5

Activities and Behavior of the Colony as an Organism

To understand behavior and activities of worker honey bees, one logical approach is to begin at the egg stage.

DEVELOPMENT

As the egg is about to hatch, it lays on its side. Workers now frequently inspect the cell and as soon as it hatches, a drop of royal jelly is deposited at the base of the cell.

Royal jelly is a secretion of the brood food glands (hypopharyngeal) of workers. In an emergency older bees can produce it; however, normally workers between 3 and 13 days secrete it. Secreting royal jelly is hard work and shortens the life of workers. This substance has been viewed as a mysterious and/or miraculous material for many generations. It has also been the subject of extensive research beginning in 1852. It has also been exploited by imaginative (or unscrupulous) individuals selling it as a miraculous cure for practically every ailment. Royal jelly has been added to lotions and cosmetics and used as a dietary supplement.

Some beekeepers look upon royal jelly as yet another marketable product bees might produce. Inoue and Inoue (1964) summarized the world market situation. At that time (1962) many beekeepers were apparently optimistic regarding the future sales potential. Greatest hindrance to expanded sales was the fact that no one has data to substantiate its therapeutic values. In Italy, royal jelly is sold in a variety of forms such as a water-alcohol solution, lyophilized, a 1-100 mixture in honey, and injectable. Regulatory agencies to date have not been convinced of its attributes other than the fact that it is a bee food.

Analysis indicates royal jelly to be a complex mixture consisting of 66% moisture, 12.34% protein, 5.46% lipids, 12.5% reducing substances, 0.82% ash, and 2.8% undetermined substances. It contains vitamins, sugars, sterols, a number of specific fatty acids, and an antibiotic 10-hydroxydecanoic acid. It is quite logical that royal jelly should contain an antibiotic since it is a nutritious material.

For about the first two days the newly hatched larva appears to swim in royal jelly. By the third day, cells appear to have less surplus food; however, visits by workers are just as frequent. Various estimates are given for the number of times the larvae must be fed—up to 1,300 visits per day or 10,000 during its lifetime. Lindauer (1953) estimates that the labor required for rearing one larva from egg to capping of the cell involves 2,785 bees, 10 hours, 16 minutes, and 8 seconds—a rather intensive labor operation.

Larvae go through five stages (instars) of growth, shedding their cuticles each time. When fully mature, other workers cap the cell with a porous material made from bits of beeswax and other materials found in the hive. Some refer to the sealed brood and pupal stage as the resting period, although developmentally the larva is by no means resting. It spins its cocoon, molts, and transforms from larva to pupa. The fully formed pupa sheds the larval cuticle, but externally no dramatic changes are visible. Larval tissue dissolves and adult tissue develops. When development is complete, the pupal shell splits and the adult bee emerges head first, using the mandibles to chew away the cap of the cell. Additional information on the embryology of the honey bee can be found in Snodgrass (1956).

TABLE 5.1. DEVELOPMENTAL TIME FOR HONEY BEES

Stage	Day		
	Worker	Queen	Drone
Egg	2½-3	2½-3	2½-3
Immature larva	4	4	4
Mature larva gorging food	2	2	3
Pre pupal	2	1	4
Pupa	9	5	8
Sealed brood	12	7½	13½
Egg to adult	20-21	14-15	22-24
Life expectancy	weeks to months	years	months

Differentiation of the honey bee into castes has intrigued biologists for many years. There are only two castes—workers and queens. While a worker's duty changes with age and colony needs, this one caste is able to take care of such necessities of life as feeding, thermo-regulation, foraging, and defense. Caste differentiation is determined by nutrition. All newly hatched fertilized eggs have the potential of becoming either a queen or a worker. All larvae are fed an identical diet of royal jelly for the first 2.5 days. Those destined to become queens are fed the same diet for an additional 2.5 days, while those who are to become workers are fed a less nutritious diet of pollen and honey. Changes that occur during this second 2.5-day period in the developing queen were viewed as miraculous by beekeepers years ago and are the basis for some folklore.

While differentiation has been researched extensively, there are unanswered questions. It is a complex process not controlled by a specific factor or factors, but apparently several working together. One hypothesis tested was that workers are the result of deliberate undernourishing of larvae after the third day, or the queen is a product of lavish feeding all during the unsealed portion of larval development, which then interferes with endocrine function of ovaries. Experimental results, however, are inconclusive. The majority usually die in the advanced pupal stage. Those that survive are intermediate between queen and worker; some resemble workers, and others the normal queen. It has also been demonstrated that the age of the larva at the time of differential feeding is an important factor in determining the kind of queen. A normal queen will be produced if differential feeding begins before the larva is three days old. If the larva is older, the queen will be imperfect. By selecting larvae for queen development based on age alone, it is possible to obtain inter castes. The amount and type of nutrition influence the quality of a queen. She has the potential to develop about 200 ovarioles; under good conditions about 180 of these become functional. However, when a queen is produced under less than ideal conditions, such as in a very small colony, about 120 develop. Such queens would be naturally replaced in the colony at an earlier date.

EMERGENCE OF THE ADULT

When development is complete, the pupal shell splits and the adult bee emerges head first using the mandibles to chew away the cap of the cell. Activities of bees have been observed by interested individuals for many years. Behavior is governed by needs of the colony as well as physiological age of the bee. Early reports indicated that newly hatched bees were relegated to cleaning cells. More recent studies indicate that bees ranging in age from 1 to 25 days will clean cells if required for the good of the colony. The same is true of feeding larvae. Most workers can feed larvae, if they have to be fed. Newly emerged bees usually feed older larvae, and once they attain the age of six days they are capable of feeding newly hatched larvae. At about three weeks their activities become generalized, doing what is needed, and now, weather permitting, they engage in play flight. This is basically an orientation flight. They leave the colony and hover within 0.91 to 1.52 meters (3 to 5 feet) of the hive entrance, facing toward the entrance, apparently imprinting on their nervous system a view of their home. It is not uncommon for young workers to drift from their colony to another adjoining one, especially if the hives are next to each other and similar in appearance. If drifting is equal in all directions, no serious problem occurs; however, such is not the case in most bee yards. Honey bees will tend to drift from a smaller colony to a larger one. If colonies are in an area where wind is always from the same direction, those colonies downwind will end up with larger populations. To reduce drift, beekeepers have painted designs and patterns of various types on hives, hoping to give their bees a better orientation or reference pattern. There are differences of opinions as to whether this helps reduce drift. Beekeepers with a large number of similar appearing hives sometimes break the continuous and repetitive pattern by facing entrances preferably south, or southeast, but not all in the exact same direction.

TEMPERATURE REGULATION

One feature of the honey bee colony which enables it to survive in adverse climates is its ability to regulate temperature. It survives, regardless of outside temperature, provided food (honey) is available. In this respect the honey bee colony resembles birds and mammals more closely than other insects. The brood area is maintained between 33° and 35°C (92° and 95°F). For this reason larval development proceeds at a predictable rate. In summer the area is cooled by fanning and water evaporation. When the surrounding air temperature drops to 14°C (57°F), bees form a cluster. By metabolizing honey and thoracic muscle movements they are able to generate heat. The tightness of the cluster regulates the temperature with bees acting as generators and insulators. While the colony can survive adverse conditions, individual bees are quite helpless in dealing with climate. They cannot fly when their body temperature drops below 10°C (50°F), lose the power to move at 5°C (42°F), and freeze at −1.9°C (28.5°F). In order to survive, the honey bee cluster temperature cannot drop below 7°C (44°F). The winter broodless cluster temperature ranges between 20° and 36°C (68° and 96°F) with the normal about 29°C (85°F).

As the temperature surrounding the cluster decreases, honey bees around the edge extend their wings forming a cover which prevents heat loss, and at the same time perform frequent and quick movements with the thorax. As the temperature drops lower, they bury their heads and

TABLE 5.2. MINIMUM AND/OR APPROXIMATE TEMPERATURE AT WHICH THE
FOLLOWING EVENTS OCCUR

| Temperature | | |
C°	F°	Activity or Event
38	100	Workers forage for water
33-35	91-95	Normal brood rearing
33-36	91-97	Wax secretion
29	85	Broodless winter cluster
20	68	Queen refuses to fly out to mate
16	61	Drones refuse to fly outside
14	57	Workers form a cluster
10	50	Workers cannot fly
5	42	Lose ability to move
5	42	Workers begin dropping from cluster
−2	28	Freeze to death

thoraxes into the cluster with their abdomens exposed. If one listens
closely by placing the ear against the surface of the upper part of the
hive, it is possible to hear the constant low-pitched buzzing hum of bees,
indicating "all is well" as long as the cluster has honey. Moisture which
results from metabolizing honey escapes the cluster; some condenses as
frost on the inner wall of the hive. As temperature moderates some will
melt and be utilized by bees. The cluster tends to slowly move upward,
usually ending at the top by spring. Bees which left the cluster intentionally, or otherwise, drop, die, and accumulate in the lower part of the
hive.

SECRETION OF WAX AND BUILDING COMB

Many people have been fascinated by the honey bee's ability to secrete
wax and build comb. Beeswax is secreted by four pairs of glands on the
ventral side of the abdomen. They are fully functional when the worker
is between 12 and 18 days old.

In an emergency, younger and older ones also can produce beeswax, but
not as efficiently. Wax is secreted during relatively high temperature—
33° to 36°C (92° to 98°F). Workers about to secrete wax engorge with
honey and hang in clusters at or near the place where comb is to be
constructed. In about 24 to 36 hours, wax flakes can be seen on the
ventral side of the abdomen. One flake is taken off at a time with the
hind leg, brought forward, and then is grasped with the mandibles and

front leg while she stands on her two center legs and one hind leg. She chews the flake and adds secretions from the mandibular glands. This secretion plus pigments from pollen give wax its yellowish color. Flakes picked off the abdomen, without being chewed, are distinctly lighter. Also, wax secreted by workers held in confinement and fed only sugar water is lighter than normal. The bees do not follow a definite cycle or pattern when removing wax scales from their bodies and fixing it to comb. Watching an individual worker bee work would lead one to believe that they are rather inefficient. It is not unusual for one worker to install a piece of wax and another one come along and move it to another area. However, the job at hand gets done. Comb is usually started at the top of the cavity and built downward, obviously in reponse to gravity. There is some evidence to suggest that honey bees also detect magnetism— constructing comb generally oriented in the north-south direction when given free choice. Being opportunists, honey bees will utilize an "artificial" base on which to construct cells, if one is provided. Beekeepers capitalize on this characteristic and provide them with wax foundation

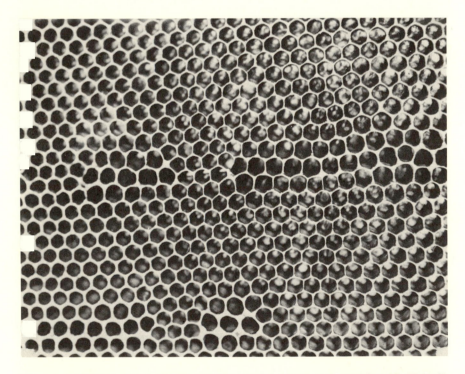

FIG. 5.1. WORKER AND LARGER DRONE CELLS. NOTE THE IRREGULAR TRANSITION COMB

held in a frame, and this is the basis of the movable frame used by beekeepers.

Wax secretion is energy-intensive, as illustrated by experiments where workers were forced to build comb but not provided with pollen as food. They lost up to 20% of their body weight in 15 days, apparently drawing on body reserves. While there is some variation, the average colony uses about 3.62 kg (8 lb) of sugar or honey to produce 0.453 kg (1 lb) of wax.

Combs constructed by honey bees have been studied by philosophers and engineers, and they agree that its basic design cannot be improved. Bees devote considerable time and effort to building comb. In the interest of efficiency, they want to obtain maximum usage with the least amount of material used. That each worker or drone cell can be used for food storage or as a nursery is one indication of efficiency. The hexagonal shape is another feature to note. While less construction material is used if round cells are made, the fact that cell walls are used in common changes the situation. While square cells would then be the design of choice, it is possible through a series of mathematical calculations to prove that hexagonal cells are the strongest possible design, when there

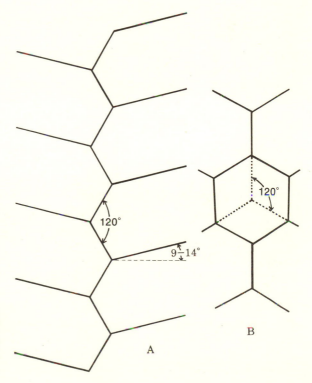

FIG. 5.2. (A) DIAGRAM SHOWING ANGLE OF CELL CONSTRUCTION. (B) DIAGRAM SHOWING SPACE-SAVING HEXA-GONAL SHAPE OF CELL

are common walls, which requires the least amount of wax. The base of each cell consists of three rhomboids which form an inverted pyramid. Each of the three rhomboids forms one-third of the base of a cell on the opposite side of the comb. Combs are built vertically and cells horizontally, sloping towards the base between 9° and 14°. While it seems logical that the cell would slope inward so that the larva does not slide out, combs can be placed upside down in the hive and bees will use them. The base of a newly constructed cell is 0.0889 mm (0.0035 in.) thick, and walls 0.0635 mm (0.0025 in.) thick. As cells are reused for brood, the walls thicken and strengthen—not by additional wax, but by the last pupal skin which remains in the cell. After repeated uses, the interior is somewhat smaller. When the cell becomes too small, workers will enlarge it by removing the pupal skins. So a comb lasts indefinitely, unless broken or damaged.

COMMUNICATIONS

If an organism is unable to communicate, it lives a solitary life; so the very existence of a social organization implies a means of communication. This does not necessarily mean that it has a language, nor does it imply that the individual is merely responding to stimuli. Essentially, communication means a transfer of information from one individual to another receptive one within the same species who is able to respond. While the human tendency is to associate communication with sound and sight, there is no valid reason why the honey bee colony could not have evolved its own system depending on odor, pheromones, touch, sound, and perhaps electrical and magnetic stimuli.

It was in 1788 that M.J.E. Spitzner suggested that honey bees, by means of a dance, communicated the volume and location of nectar sources to others in the colony. *"When a bee has come upon a good supply of honey anywhere, on her return home she makes this known in a peculiar way to others. Full of joy she twists in circles about those in the hive from above, downward and from below upward so that they shall surely notice the smell of honey on her; for many of them soon follow when she goes out again. I observed this in the glassed hive when I put some honey not far away on the grass and brought only two of the bees to it. In a few minutes since these had made it known to others in the manner described they came in great numbers to the place"* (von Frisch 1967). Spitzner's observations were either ignored or overlooked until Karl von Frisch published his initial observations on the subject in 1920. Von Frisch's first papers were concerned with fish and their sensory perception, and later changed to honey bees. His early studies were related to perception of color, taste, and smell, and in 1945, first as-

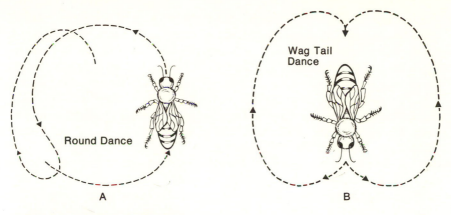

FIG. 5.3. HONEY BEE DANCES

(A) Round: Indicates food is available, but no direction is given. (B) Wag tail: Gives direction. See Fig. 5.4.

sociated what he called the wag-tail dance with distance and direction to the source of nectar. Von Frisch described two types of movements that a returning worker performs after a successful foraging trip. He called one the round dance and the other the wag-tail dance. In the round dance the worker, with quick short steps, runs in a narrow circle, often changing direction to the right, then to the left. She does this for several seconds or up to a minute, then may move to another part of the comb, and finally to the entrance to return to the source for more. The round dance is performed when the food source is less than 100 meters (300 ft) from the colony. No information is given as to how far away it might be.

If the food source is farther than 100 meters (300 ft), then returning workers perform the wag-tail dance. She makes a narrow half-circle to one side, then a sharp turn and runs in a straight line to the starting point, and makes another half-circle in the opposite direction, thus completing a full circle. When running in the straight line, she vigorously shakes her abdomen sideways. This movement von Frisch called the wag-tail dance. During the straight run, low frequency sound waves are produced and can be correlated with distance to the food source (Wenner 1964). Von Frisch was able to correlate the number of straight runs per 15-second period with distance. For example, if food was 600 meters (1968 ft) away, returning worker made 7 straight runs; if 6,000 meters (19,680 ft), 2 runs during this 15-second period. If the source of food is towards the sun, the straight run is upward, away from gravity; if away, then downward. Locations to the right or left of the sun are indicated by deviations of the straight run from the vertical. While the sun is used as a reference, the eye of the honey bee is capable of detecting polarized and

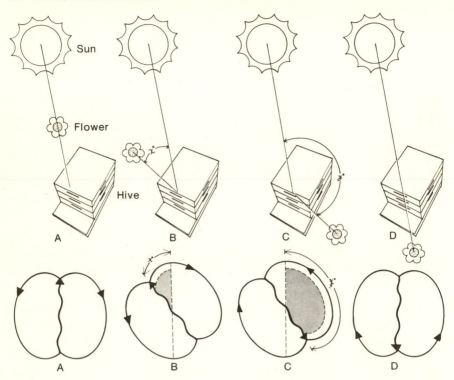

FIG. 5.4. FORAGING WORKER HONEY BEE COMMUNICATING DIRECTION USING THE SUN AS A REFERENCE: (A) DIRECTLY TOWARDS THE SUN; (B) TO LEFT OF THE SUN X°; (C) TO THE RIGHT OF THE SUN Y°; (D) DIRECTLY AWAY FROM THE SUN

ultraviolet light, so she need not see the sun to navigate, as the plane of polarization is correlated with the position of the sun. Adjustments or corrections for wind, hills, and valleys appear to be made automatically.

Returning workers have no way to communicate "up" and "down." If the source of food were on a mountainside or in a valley, under natural conditions this would pose no specific problem. Recruited workers would undoubtedly find the source by following the contours. However, should the food be placed on a high tower or building, recruited workers would not find it.

Worker honey bees also perform other dances which communicate information useful to the colony. For example, mixing dinitrocresol with sugar-syrup will cause bees to run in spirals and in irregular patterns and vigorously shake their abdomens. Neighboring bees respond by stopping flight activity. These movements have been entitled the alarm dance. To remove dust and debris, some workers will perform a cleaning or grooming dance—apparently asking others to help clean up.

Returning workers also communicate odors to others in the hive. These would be in the nectar as well as on the waxy cuticle of the worker's body. The quantity of food available is communicated by the number of dancing bees in the hive and the frequency of dances. A short loading time would suggest an abundant supply, so the interval between dances is short. Hazards associated with foraging are indirectly communicated. A worker encountering something highly toxic would probably die before returning. A slower acting poison might cause her to get lost, or if the material had a peculiar odor, guard bees may not let her inside the hive.

For his contribution to the understanding of honey bee communication, von Frisch was awarded the Nobel prize in 1973. He succeeded not only in breaking the honey bee code, but was very successful in communicating his findings to the public by selecting easily understood and imaginative terms, and also vividly describing how he proceeded to answer simple questions. For example, he used terms such as "language of the bees," "wag-tail dance," and "round dance" which are easily understood. His book is highly recommended to anyone interested in this subject (von Frisch 1967). He also stimulated many others to investigate the fascinating subject of communication. For a more comprehensive treatment of the subject a publication by Lindauer (1971) is recommended.

Von Frisch's work on honey bee communication is not beyond question (Wenner 1971). Part of the criticism is based on von Frisch's choice of words: dance and language. Wenner feels there should be a distinction between language and communication. The mere presence of a signal between members of a species does not mean that they have a language. Wenner prefers to define language as the means by which species transmit and use symbolic information from one to another. The receiving individual must be able to evaluate and use the information. The fact that returning field bees perform a dance in the hive is not questioned, but Wenner stresses that correlation does not imply causality. The fact that the worker performs some movements does not prove that she is transmitting direction and distance information. The charge made is that von Frisch ignored production and transmission of sound. Could not the foraging bee lay down an odor over and around the area where nectar and pollen were produced, and now she is telling other field bees to go out and search for the center of this pattern? Von Frisch states that as the concentration of nectar increases, the vigor and intensity of the dance increase. Wenner feels that von Frisch's explanation does not quantify the concentration of nectar, and he also feels many of von Frisch's hypotheses are being interpreted as facts.

FORAGING FOR NECTAR AND POLLEN

When a honey bee worker becomes three weeks old, she can begin foraging for pollen, nectar, or water, depending on weather and the needs of the colony. If a worker starts collecting pollen, there is a good chance that she will stay with this activity for at least 3 or 4 consecutive days, and may stay with the same plant species for up to 20 days. If a plant produces pollen or secretes nectar at a specific time of the day, she will adjust her schedule to it. While it is customary for a honey bee to work one species at a time, there are exceptions. About 3 to 10% of the returning field bees will bring in a mixed load of pollen. Most workers seem to confine their foraging activities to a specific geographic area, although it is difficult to obtain precise data to verify this opinion. Undoubtedly, this will vary with availability of plants, prevailing winds, and barriers such as forests. Foragers seldom venture out when the temperature is lower than 8°C (46°F). They travel an average of 24 km per hour (15 mph) on the return home trip, but fly out at a more variable rate ranging between 10 and 29 km per hour (6 and 18 mph). Although most will forage between 1 and 3 km (½ and 2 miles) from the hive, they will if necessary travel up to 12 km (7½ miles). The foraging area is not a perfect circle around the hive, but will vary with availability of plants.

A foraging trip may take from six minutes to three hours. She may visit 8 to 100 blossoms, bring between 12 and 29 mg (0.0042 and 0.0102 oz) pollen back home, and may make 6 to 47 trips per day. Obviously, there is considerable variation, and individual behavior will be governed greatly by circumstances such as availability and condition of plants, and distance from the hive. About 25% of the field bees bring home pollen, 58 to 60% return with only nectar, and the others return with a combined load.

Upon returning to the hive the honey bee worker performs her dance several times, locates a suitable cell, examines it with her head and antenna, turns around and backs into it and dislodges the pellets from the pollen basket. This behavior is instinctive. If pollen pellets are dislodged from her legs at the hive entrance, she will perform the same ritual of the dance, examining a cell and backing into it, even though the pellets were absent.

House bees now push the pellets to the base of the cell with their heads, then use the mandibles to level and pack it. If the material appears dry, it will be moistened with nectar. The material will undergo a fermentation quite similar to chopped corn in a silo.

Nectar foraging is not dramatically different from hunting for pollen. In some cases she must insert the proboscis into the flower to determine if some is present. In other situations she can depend on vision to locate nectar. It is well documented that the honey bee sees three primary colors, yellow, blue and ultraviolet, but not red. Photographs taken with a camera equipped with a quartz lens and red filter indicate that nectar droplets on some plants are conspicuously visible, so locating nectar may not be as difficult for the honey bee as was once believed.

Foraging workers probably leave an odor when visiting a flower, because other bees appear to avoid a recently visited blossom. As with pollen foraging, precise data are difficult to obtain, and considerable variation in behavior can be expected because of environmental conditions. A worker will visit 1 to 1,400 flowers per trip. If she can obtain a full load from less than 100 blossoms, nectar production is considered good. A foraging trip may last from 25 minutes to 2.5 hours. Some will make up to 24 trips per day, others as few as 7 per day. A load of nectar can weigh from 25 to 70 mg (0.0087 to 0.0245 oz), averaging 40 mg (0.014 oz). Generally, heavier loads are carried during hot weather and if the sugar concentration is higher.

Upon returning to the hive, the honey bee worker will distribute her load to three or four house bees, making contact with the antennae and front legs. She regurgitates the materials which form a droplet around the base of the proboscis and mandibles. The house bees ingest it with their proboscis so the material is transferred without spilling a drop. The field worker then cleans her proboscis with her front legs, runs the antenna through the notch on the front leg, which cleans it, and takes off for another load.

Once the house bee obtains her full load, she moves to a less crowded area of the hive. Facing upward, she begins a series of manipulations with her mandibles and proboscis to actively evaporate moisture and blend nectar with the enzyme invertase, which splits sucrose into glucose and fructose. The contents of the crop (honey stomach) are slowly regurgitated. It hangs as a small flat droplet from the mandibles, and the proboscis is now lowered to expose the nectar to the air, thereby evaporating moisture. She may do this for as long as 20 minutes, but for a shorter period if nectar is coming in rapidly.

When this house bee is ready to deposit the unripened honey into a cell, she crawls in, ventral side up, and regurgitates the material. Using the proboscis as a brush, she paints this nectar on the upper side of the cell. This material runs down the sides and collects at the base. If she enters a cell which already contains some honey, she merely lowers her proboscis into it and adds her load. When nectar comes in slowly, it is deposited in a large number of cells, but only 25% are filled, so moisture evaporates faster. Moisture content of nectar varies considerably, ranging from 5 to 80% sugars. For a long time, it was thought that the water loss from the collected material began in the honey stomach during the return flight home. It has been shown, however, that this organ is impermeable to water so the contents are a little more diluted on return to the hive than it was at the source of feeding. Dilution is due to the addition of saliva, so all of the moisture has to be evaporated at the hive. Some moisture is lost at the time that it is transferred within the hive, and the remainder has to be evaporated from the cells by air currents. The faster nectar arrives from the field, the less moisture is evaporated before storage. If space is available between combs, workers readily add extensions to the partly filled, uncapped cells. As soon as the moisture content of honey drops to 20%, workers seal the cell with a thin layer of wax, providing it with an air-tight cover.

FORAGING FOR WATER AND PROPOLIS

Honey bee workers also forage for water when nectar is not available and during hot weather when it is necessary to cool the interior of the hive. Returning foragers communicate distance and direction to others in the colony using the dance as they do when gathering pollen or nectar. Water is not stored in the hive in any appreciable amounts, but certain workers will keep it in their crop (honey stomach) and thus serve as a water reservoir, distributing it to others on an as needed basis. When moisture is needed to prevent larvae from desiccation, a small drop is placed inside the cell or on the surface of the capped cell of sealed brood.

A few workers in each colony collect propolis, especially during hot weather. Propolis is a glue-like resin secreted by some plants. Upon locating a source, the worker bites it off with its mandibles, and with the help of the first pair of legs, kneads it, then transfers the material to the pollen basket. This entire operation may require 15 to 60 minutes. Upon entering the hive, another worker removes it from her legs, manipulates it with her mandibles, sometimes adding a bit of wax. This material is then carried to a place where it is needed, and if there are no urgent needs, it is added to a piece of existing propolis. The percentage of bees foraging for propolis is very low, but when a specific worker locates a source or begins foraging for it, she remains with this activity for a relatively long time. There are considerable differences among colonies as to the amount of propolis collected. The Caucasian race of honey bees has the reputation of being prolific gatherers of it.

ROBBING

Robbing is an activity that can be considered as a special type of foraging. The honey bee is an opportunist and will seek nectar, sugar syrup, or honey of highest concentration. Most honey contains some aromatic materials which scout bees readily locate. Upon returning to the hive with this honey, others are recruited and robbing is underway. The most likely victims of robbing are small or weak colonies, especially those with large entrances which cannot be defended. Some writers apologize for the name "robber," stating creatures such as honey bees have no criminal intent and therefore should not be called robber bees. Others describe the behavior of robbers as acting nervously, and showing signs of guilt.

Robbers go directly for honey, ignoring guards and defenders, and even the queen. There are casualties on both sides. The defenders attack by biting at the wings and legs of the intruders, and often engage them in direct battle by stinging. The queen and unsealed larvae will perish in a short time due to starvation. The uninformed beekeeper may be unconcerned if his bees are robbing some unfortunate victim. However, this is the primary way in which disease is spread. A diseased colony becomes weak and cannot defend itself. The disease organism is in the honey, so when it is brought into the strong, healthy colony, it too is infected and so the disease is perpetuated.

FANNING

Air currents are used to evaporate moisture from open cells. On warm days when nectar is rapidly coming in, honey bee workers will arrange themselves in front of 25 to 50% of the entrance to the hive. They face inward, spaced so that their wings do not touch when extended sideways, and then rapidly move them (180 to 195 times per minute) to push air outward. The thrust is approximately one-third greater than the weight of a honey bee, so she must grasp on to the surface or be blown away. This sets up an air flow that ranges between 57 to 90 meters per minute (187 to 295 ft per minute), averaging 78 meters per minute (256 ft per minute). In extreme conditions, others will take a similar position on the opposite side of the entrance. They face outward, forcing air in. This not only evaporates moisture from the honey, but cools the hive.

Honey bees will also fan when exposing Nassanoff's gland (scent gland). Secretions are used to orientate bees to their hive or cluster. If a large number of workers is intentionally or accidentally dislodged a short distance (1 meter) from the hive, other workers will face toward the hive, flex their abdomens, and begin fanning. This behavior establishes an odor gradient, and in a short time all workers (even those who never before ventured from the hive) start moving to their colony.

SWARMING

Swarming is a natural event by which a colony reproduces. Factors governing swarming are complex and not completely understood. While it is the strong healthy colonies which swarm, this phenomenon is also influenced by photoperiod, genetics, physical crowdings, and the age of the queen. Old queens have a greater tendency to swarm than young ones. In the northern hemisphere, swarming takes place beginning in late February in southern Florida, and ending by July 1 in northern areas. While there are exceptions, in the interest of species survival and perpetuation, it is only logical that swarming be regulated. A late swarm would not have time to gather and store enough nectar and pollen before winter and would surely die.

In northern areas, swarms which emerged in May and early June have an excellent opportunity to survive if the weather is near normal, since they will have gathered sufficient nectar and pollen to last through the winter.

Signs of swarming are evident at least seven to ten days before the

FIG. 5.5. NORMAL BROOD PATTERN AND CUP CELLS

event happens. Building of queen cup cells on the lower sides of the comb, in the lower part of the brood nest, is the first signal, although many colonies will build cup cells, but will not swarm. Cup cells will become the base of the queen cell.

To better understand the natural process of swarming, this discussion will start with the queen's egg laying pattern. Young bees have a tendency to stay on the comb, in the center of the cluster, or on combs in the vicinity of where they developed. As numbers of new bees increase, older ones are forced outward. As they are "pushed" outward, they begin to clean cells. As the queen moves across these freshly cleaned cells, she deposits an egg in each that is ready. Other young bees feed the queen and newly hatched larvae. As the swarming season approaches, the rate of egg laying increases. Under normal conditions, a queen has about 10 to 12 nurse bees attending to her needs. As the egg laying tempo increases, additional workers join the retinue and offer her more food so she may have up to 20 attendants and is laying eggs at a very rapid rate (up to 1,500 eggs per day).

Field workers are also gathering nectar and pollen and eventually all the cells contain nectar, pollen, or brood. The queen now seeks out the queen cup cells (swarm cells) and deposits an egg in each. The fact that she has no place to lay eggs and the general crowding of the hive signals other workers to reduce feeding her, or she accepts less food, and her abdomen begins to shrink. About this time, the majority of the larvae are sealed and no longer require feeding, so many of the young workers are "unemployed." Because of crowding, field workers tend to reduce foraging and also stay home. These conditions signal some to begin looking for a new home, and others to keep their crops filled with honey.

Normally, after the developing queen cell is capped, and on a warm sunny day usually between 10 AM and 2 PM, a large number (no fixed percentage) will rapidly leave the hive, hover in the immediate vicinity and then move away toward some object like a post or tree. Since the queen has lost about 30% of her weight, and the abdomen is greatly reduced, she is able to fly along with the swarm. The majority of the workers in the swarm will be between 4 and 23 days old, although sometimes younger and older ones will also accompany it. A few workers will land on some resting site and begin emitting a scent from Nassanoff's gland. This attracts others who in turn will do the same thing, and eventually the whole swarm comes to rest. During this episode, the queen acts like a worker by following the swarm instead of leading it. If she is prevented from following the swarm or gets lost, the swarm will return to its hive. Bees that are not engorged with honey will also leave the swarm and return home. Workers who assumed responsibility or delegated themselves as scouts are out searching for a new home which could be any suitable cavity.

Honey bees have a hierarchy of preferences in selecting their future home. They will occupy a wooden box in preference to a straw skep, an area protected from wind in preference to one out in the open, a site some distance away rather than one nearby, a hive entrance exposed to the sun rather than one in deep shade. Scouts, on returning to the swarm, will "try to convince" the swarm of the merits of the home they have located. They communicate not only direction and distance with their wag-tail dance, but the quality of the new site. The more intense the dance, the better the home. If several scouts return from sites in different areas, which are of "questionable merits," the swarm will probably remain stationary. If, on the other hand, a number of scouts returned with information that a highly desirable site was available, the swarm would take off and occupy it. If the "decision is not unanimous and convincing," the swarm can and will split and later reunite.

There are limits on the time period over which a colony can swarm. While the swarm can stay in the hive for several days to wait out a rainy or cold spell of weather, prolonged periods require adjustments. The emerging queen can be "put in hold" for a limited time within her own cell. She will delay emergence if workers feed her before she crawls out, thus giving additional time for the old queen to leave.

It is not unusual for several swarms to emerge from a single large colony. The one which contains the old queen is referred to as a primary swarm, others as secondary. Secondary swarms are usually accompanied by an unmated queen or queens. Presumably, after this swarm is settled in its new home, she will fly out, mate, return to kill her rivals, and on with the job of laying eggs.

The old queen which accompanied the swarm will begin laying as soon as workers have constructed sufficient comb. Some believe she will be superceded shortly, allowing the new colony to raise its own queen.

The general public is terrified of swarms and is also impressed by the bravery of a beekeeper who is able to capture one. Honey bees in a swarm are gentle and can be handled with ease. The reason is quite simple as honey bees are not aggressive, but defensive. A colony is temporarily without a home, hence there is nothing to defend. But, as with all behavioral traits, there are exceptions. If the swarm is not able to find a suitable hive and has been in the same location for several days, things can change. Workers begin to exhaust their food reserve in the crop; or they may consider their present resting site as their home and begin to defend it even though it is not inside a cavity. Capturing such a swarm sometimes will involve a few stings.

QUEENLESS COLONY

Shortly after a colony becomes queenless, workers start building queen cells. However, should queenlessness occur when eggs or young larvae are not present, the colony is then said to be hopelessly queenless, destined to perish. Workers in such a colony become more defensive, and experienced beekeepers often recognize it as soon as it is opened for inspection.

Worker honey bees have a natural tendency to cluster even in the absence of a queen. Normally, even a few workers will cluster around a queen, but before queenless honey bees form a cluster, a critical mass or number is required. If 75 or more honey bees are in a group, they will form a cluster, especially if the temperature is reduced. If this mass is reduced to about 50 workers or less, clustering may not take place, but they may congregate in small groups of 3 or 4. Within the larger cluster a division of labor will develop, such as comb building, nectar and pollen gathering, and other activities which proceed, but at a greatly reduced rate. Some nectar and pollen will be stored below the brood area rather than above, as in a normal colony.

The presence of a queen and developing larvae suppresses ovary development in workers, so it is not unusual for laying workers to develop in a queenless colony. But laying workers will develop on occasion in a queen-right colony, especially one preparing to swarm. Eggs produced by laying workers would develop into drones. A laying worker adopts a few behavioral traits of a queen, but retains most of her worker characteristics. For example, she will eat pollen and honey and even fly outside.

She inspects the cell before laying just like a queen, but if it is not ready she will attempt to clean it. When depositing an egg, she usually turns the ventral side of her body to the side rather than to the lower surface of the cell. Nor is she accorded the same attention as a queen. While workers form a crude circle around her, it is much less organized, and not as stable as one formed around a laying queen.

In queenless colonies usually a number of laying workers develop simultaneously. While each lays only one egg per cell, this does not prevent others from using the same cell, so often the brood area has many cells, each containing several eggs.

As soon as eggs begin to hatch, workers show aggression towards the laying workers by driving them about the hive.

COLONY DEFENSE

Everybody knows that bees sting and that it is a rather unpleasant encounter. Some enthusiastic beekeepers minimize the significance of the stinger, insisting it is only 1.5 mm ($\frac{1}{16}$ in.) long; the rest is anticipation and imagination. While the results of a sting are dramatic and obvious, other factors involved in colony defense are highly complex and not thoroughly understood.

The honey bee (and all social hymenoptera) stings only to defend its home. Some believe the sting is a carry-over from a more primitive ancestor which injected venom to paralyze the host, then deposited an egg inside its body. The disabled carcass serves as food for the developing larva. While solitary wasps can sting, they rarely cause problems in man. Others postulate that the stinging mechanism evolved independently, and use as evidence the chemical components of venom which are extremely toxic to birds and mammals. There is no logical reason for such a toxic material to evolve if it were only to be used against other insects. However, there is no question that the stinger is a modified ovipositor. Needless to say, the stinger is a formidable weapon of defense and the honey bee will challenge any intruder, regardless of size.

The number of honey bees defending a colony varies considerably during the course of a season. During nectar flow, fewer workers are relegated to defense than when nectar is not available. But the number committed to defense also depends on other factors. For example, if the hive is disturbed by tapping or opening, many will abandon their work and take defensive measures. They employ zone defense at the entrance as well as around the hive. Larger intruders are challenged further away. This distance may range from 1 to 10 meters (3.2 to 32.8 feet), depending on genetics of the hive, time of year, and climatic conditions.

Guards also challenge all entering bees when nectar is not available, and will allow "foreigners" to enter only if they are carrying pollen or nectar; if not, they are turned away. A guarding honey bee stands on the second and third pair of legs with the first pair lifted, and the antennae extended forward. Identification is undoubtedly by odor. Intruders are turned back, and if they refuse several guards will pounce on them, biting at the wings and legs and making attempts to sting. Other insects such as wasps and bumble bees sometimes either attempt to gain entrance, or accidentally stray too near the hive entrance. The more fortunate are able to escape, but it is not unusual to find a dead one in the immediate vicinity of a colony, a victim of an effective defensive system.

Temperament or disposition is used to describe a colony's defensive behavior. A colony is said to have a gentle temperament when its workers are less reluctant to sting than those from another colony which is handled in a similar fashion. For years beekeepers routinely eliminated highly defensive colonies by introducing queens from more gentle stock. Some queen producers also tend to eliminate highly defensive ones from their line. Controlled breeding at research institutions suggests that defensiveness is an inherited characteristic controlled by multiple factors. While no one has developed or selected a stingless honey bee, there are those who feel that this would not be desirable. However, it is possible to have highly defensive colonies or very gentle ones and all gradations between.

Environmental conditions affect the disposition of the colony. Workers are more defensive on cloudy days or if the colony is located in a deeply shaded area. The colony is more defensive in the fall after the nectar flow than in the spring. The color of the intruder affects the colony. They will strike at a black or red colored object before a light one, and they will readily strike at a shining article or fast-moving object. The wrist watch and eye glasses are favorite targets. Beekeepers are able to capitalize on these behavioral characteristics by wearing light-colored clothes, removing wrist watches or wearing protective gloves, and they quickly learn to avoid quick movements around the hive.

Pheromones are also important in colony defense. Isopentyl acetate has been identified as an alarm pheromone that is released when a worker stings or is accidentally crushed. This chemical incites others to strike or sting in the immediate vicinity. For this reason, it is not unusual for an individual manipulating a colony to receive several stings immediately after accidentally crushing a honey bee.

Immediately after the stinger penetrates the skin, venom is injected into the wound. The initial reaction is intense pain followed by localized swelling, which is the normal and anticipated reaction. The severity of the pain and intensity of the swelling will depend on the quantity and depth to which the venom was injected. Not all parts of the body respond to a sting in an identical manner. Areas around the eyes and lips tend to swell more severely than others. Medically, insect stings have been classified into three categories. *Hymenoptera vulgaris* (1) is the most common reaction. There is pain, swelling, and possibly stiffness, which may last for an hour or one or more days. Localized reddening usually occurs but disappears within several hours. The only danger would be the momentary distraction should a person be stung while driving a motor vehicle. *Hymenoptera intermedia* (2) is the classification given to a more violent reaction, probably due to the site of the sting. This reaction may not be lethal, but can be extremely painful. A sting on the lip, tongue, nose, near the eye, or even on the arm might fit this category. *Hymenoptera ultima* (3) is, of course, serious and can be lethal to some individuals if medical help is not sought immediately.

Many individuals believe that they are allergic to bees and wasps when in fact they are not. Pain and swelling due to a sting are normal, but a person who is allergic has a systemic pathological disturbance rather than a localized reaction. Public health officials estimate between one and six percent of the population could be allergic to any one or all of the stinging hymenoptera. A person can be allergic to the venom, insect body parts, or both, and the medical profession can test for circulating antibodies to determine whether the individual was recently stung.

The first sting is rarely fatal to an allergic individual, but it sensitizes, and the second or third one induces anaphylactic shock which could be fatal in 30 minutes unless emergency medical treatments are administered. Most people can be desensitized with antigens. The procedure involves administering increasingly larger doses of the sensitizing antigen until the body is able to tolerate a "normal" sting without entering shock. There are differences of opinion as to whether it is best to use pure venom, whole body extracts, or extracts prepared from several species. The broader the spectrum of materials, the greater risk of introducing objectionable or damaging foreign proteins. Persons sensitive to insect body parts probably would not be desensitized by pure venom. While desensitization is an involved process, it is successful in about 90% of the cases. Once a person is desensitized, some physicians suggest that a maintenance dosage of antigen be administered every two to three weeks during the insect season and three to six weeks at other times.

The honey bee venom is a highly complex mixture of carbohydrates, lipids, free amino acids, peptides, proteins, enzymes, and about 80% water. One worker can inject between 0.05 and 0.3 ml (0.0017 and 0.0102 fl oz) of venom with a sting.

Of the eight identified proteins, five are known to be antigenic to humans, and one has no known pharmacologic activity. Its biological activity cannot be accounted for by any of the identified components alone. Bee venom is highly toxic. The LD_{50} is 1.75 mg/kg intravenous and 3.5 mg/kg subcutaneous to mice. The LD_{50} is a measure of toxicity—the lower the number, the more poisonous the material. Dried venom in saline solution injected into dogs reduced blood pressure in 35 seconds, and death is usually due to respiratory failure. Some of the identified ingredients of honey bee venom are histamine, lecithinase, hyaluronidase phospholipases, and acid phosphatase. Hyaluronidase is an enzyme which promotes internal spreading of venom. Phospholipases, which are also present in snake venom and hydrolyze lysolecithins, cause a breakdown in red blood cells and most cells which in turn release 5-hydroxytryptamine and histamine. This process causes pain and the delayed effect of the sting. Formic acid is presumably responsible for the initial pain which accompanies the sting. Melittin and apamin, which increase blood plasma cortisol, are present. This could be partly responsible for the belief by some that honey bee stings relieve some painful symptoms of arthritis. Needless to say, honey bee venom is a complex mixture.

To those who react normally to the sting, there is little to fear other than the uncomfortable swelling and pain. Those who are allergic or sensitized should be in contact with competent medical authorities as an additional sting could be fatal if they are caught unprepared. First aid insect sting kits are available by prescription, and those who do not wish to, or are unable to be desensitized, should have one available at all times during the sting season.

Statistics on deaths caused by honey bee stings are difficult to obtain. The World Health Organization tabulates mortality data and groups them into 150 categories. Deaths caused by bees and other venomous animals are not identified; however, U.S. Vital Statistics Records puts all deaths (between 40 and 50 per year) caused by venomous animals into one category, E 905. Barr (1971) reported that hymenopterous insects were responsible for 229 deaths between 1950 and 1959. Of these 124 were caused by bee stings, 101 by yellow jackets and hornets, 4 by ants, and 65 by scorpions and spiders. During this same period, snakes were responsible for 138 fatalities. It must be pointed out that far more people are exposed to hymenopterous insects than snakes. Eighty percent of the deaths due to insect stings occurred within one hour after the person was stung. Only eight deaths were caused by a massive number of stings, which indicates that the majority of fatalities is due to the allergic reaction rather than the inherent danger of the honey bee.

There is no question that man has learned a great deal about the honey bee. While he has and can observe them in many different situations, perform controlled experiments, analyze their activities and behavior, and even select for specific genetic lines, he has not been able to alter their basic behavior. Somewhat less known and understood, but equally interesting, are the more primitive social insects studied by Michener (1974). While activities and behavior of the honey bee continue to fascinate man, based on the present state of knowledge, these need not be viewed as mysterious. Unexplained phenomena are due to gaps in knowledge, and as more is learned about their true nature, more fully will they be understood.

BIBLIOGRAPHY

BARR, S.E. 1971. Allergy to hymenoptera stings, review of world literature 1953-1970. Ann. Allergy 29:49-66.

EBELING, W. 1975. Urban Entomology. Univ. of California, Div. of Agricultural Science, Los Angeles, Calif.

INOUE, T., and A. INOUE. 1964. The world royal jelly industry: present status and future prospects. Bee World 45 (2) 59-67.

LINDAUER, M. 1953. Division of labour in the honey bee colony. Bee World 34:63:73, 85-90.

LINDAUER, M. 1971. Communication Among Social Bees. Harvard University Press, Cambridge, Mass.

MICHENER, C.D. 1974. The Social Behavior of the Bees, A Comparative Study. Belknap Press, Cambridge, Mass.

PARRISH, H.M. 1963. Analysis of 460 fatalities from venomous animals in the United States. Am. J. Med. Sci. 245:129-141.

SNODGRASS, R.E. 1956. Anatomy of the Honey Bee. Comstock Publishing Associates, Cornell University Press, Ithaca, N.Y.

VON FRISCH, K. 1967. The Dance Language and Orientation of Bees. Belknap Press, Cambridge, Mass. (Translated by L.F. Chadwick)

WENNER, A.M. 1964. Sound communications in honey bees. Sci. Am. *210* (4) 116-124.

WENNER, A.M. 1971. The Bee Language Controversy. An Experience in Science Education Programs Improvement Corp., Boulder, Colo.

6

Nutrition

Honey bee nutrition is of interest not only to the scholarly research-
er, but of practical significance to the beekeeper. Intelligent management decisions can be made only when the basic nutritional requirements
of the honey bee are understood. Nutrition, in most insects with complete metamorphosis, can be treated as two completely separate entities.
Usually larval nutritional requirements are completely different from
adults'. However, with honey bees, larval and adult nutrition is closely
interrelated because adults must actively nurse-feed larvae.

Nutrition is the all-inclusive process by which an organism incorporates
the various foods, minerals, vitamins, water, and other ingredients into
body materials and obtains energy to maintain life processes. The honey
bee is no different from other organisms since it requires energy, protein,
fats, minerals, water, vitamins, etc. Energy is supplied by carbohydrates
in the form of sugars and all other dietary requirements are obtained
from pollen. Proteins are broken down into amino acids, and fats are
either absorbed directly or changed to fatty acids and glycerol. The small
molecules produced from digestion may be used to produce energy or
synthesized into tissue or food reserves. Energy is used in building organic molecules, for contracting muscles, and for transmitting nerve impulses. Muscle contraction allows the honey bee to fly, walk, sting, etc.

CARBOHYDRATES

Larval nutritional requirements are somewhat different from those of
adult honey bees. Adults can live for a relatively long time on a diet of
pure carbohydrates, but proteins are essential for larval growth and
development. Adults cannot use pollen for energy. It is not unusual to
have a cluster of bees starve with pollen available in combs when the
supply of honey is exhausted. In flight, honey bees must also have
available, and constantly replace, the supply of carbohydrates since they
cannot use body or pollen protein, or fat for energy.

Blood sugar content in a honey bee worker is about 2%. If it falls below 1%, she can move her wings but cannot fly; below 0.5%, she cannot move at all. Drones have a slightly lower blood sugar content, 1.2%, and a newly emerged queen, 1.7%, although when she is laying, blood sugar content can drop as low as 0.3%. Flying workers use about 10 mg (0.0035 oz) sugar per hour and drones about three times more. Honey bee workers caged at 11°C (52°F) will use about 11 mg (0.0038 oz) sugar per hour, at 37°C (98°F) it drops to 0.7 mg (0.000245 oz) per hour, and at 48°C (118°F) it increases to 1.4 mg (0.00049 oz) per hour. This type of carbohydrate utilization would be expected since the ability of the honey bee colony to regulate its temperature by generating and retaining heat in a cluster is critical to its survival in colder climates. The precise amount of carbohydrates used by a colony is difficult to determine. While some estimate a colony utilizes about 79.3 kg (175 lb) per year, considerable variations exist. Factors such as colony size, brood rearing, wax secretion, and prevailing temperature influence energy consumption.

TABLE 6.1.   CARBOHYDRATES NORMALLY INGESTED BY HONEY BEES AND THEIR EFFECT

DIGESTED AND USED AS SOURCE OF ENERGY
Arabinose, cellobiose, dextrins, fructose, glucose, mannitol, maltose, melezitose, a-methyl glucoside, raffinose, sorbitol, sucrose, trehalose, xylose
NOT DIGESTED
dulcitol, erythritol, fucose, lactose, melibiose, inositol sorbose
TOXIC
formose, galactose, mannose, rhamnose

Carbohydrate metabolism in honey bees probably is not dramatically different from that in other living organisms. Although honey bees lack the necessary enzymes to digest lactose, this phenomenon of a "missing" enzyme is not unusual. Bees evolved to rely on nectar and/or honey dew (an excretion by aphids) as their source of energy. Both of these materials are complex mixtures of carbohydrates. While the major constituents of nectar and honey are glucose, fructose, and sucrose, analysis indicates that many other sugars are present also. Recently published reports indicate that there are as many as 12 mono- and disaccharides, and 11 oligosaccharides present in honey. Some materials which are detected in honey may be formed from sucrose by enzyme activity and acid reversion. However, the origin and nutritional significance of some of these less commonly known naturally occurring sugars have not been established.

There are those who believe, and with good reason, that nectar is a surplus or even a waste product, produced in excess of normal plant requirements, and that it is excreted by nectaries or accumulates in some flowers. Honey bees and some other insects evolved a system of utilizing these products as a source of energy. For this reason, it would not be surprising that nectar and honeydew contain a wide variety of carbohydrates. However, experimental evidence to date suggests that carbohydrate requirements of the honey bee colony can be met by sucrose, but they can also utilize some other sugars equally well. There are also some naturally occurring sugars which cannot be utilized by honey bees and a few which are known to be toxic.

TABLE 6.2. PLANTS AS REPORTED IN LITERATURE KNOWN TO PRODUCE TOXIC NECTAR AND/OR POLLEN

Common Name	Scientific
Azalea	*Rhododendron spp.*
Black nightshade	*Solanum nigrum*
California buckeye	*Aesculus california*
Death camas	*Zygadenus venenosus*
Dodder	*Cuscuta spp.*
Henbane	*Hyoscyamus niger*
Hellebore	*Veratrum album*
Horse chestnut	*Aesculus hypocastanum*
Karaka tree	*Corynocarpus laevigata*
Leatherwood	*Cyrilla racemiflora*
Loccoweed	*Astragulus sp.*
Mountain laurel	*Kalmina latifolia*
Rhododendron	*Rhododendron sp.*
Seaside arrow grass	*Triglochin maritima*
Star jasmine	*Oleacae*
Tansy ragwort	*Senecio jacobaea*
Tutu	*Coriaria arborea*
Western false hellebore	*Veratrum californicum*
Whorled milkweed	*Asclepias subverticillata*

PROTEIN

While each animal species has its own unique nutritional requirements, it is protein which is often either the limiting or the most expensive constituent to supply, if the organism is to be managed for the benefit of mankind. This same principle is true for honey bees. Pollen supplies the colony's total protein needs which are essential for body growth, tissue repair, and other normal body functions. Pollen does not supply energy for honey bees. As far back as 1800, some beekeepers recognized the importance of pollen to the welfare of the colony. They observed that brood rearing stopped in two or three weeks after pollen supply was exhausted.

The honey bee's instinctive behavior to gather pollen is highly developed. If pollen is in short supply in the colony and if weather permits, workers will fly out and gather many non-digestible materials such as road and coal dust, sawdust, rotten wood, and ground animal feed. Pollen has two functions in the operation of a normal colony. It is eaten by newly emerged adults as a source of protein, vitamins, minerals, and fats, which enable the brood food glands to develop normally. Brood food glands in nurse bees secrete a nutritious substance, royal jelly, which is high in protein and is fed to the newly hatched larvae and queen. Pollen is used also as a direct source of protein, fed to older larvae and drones. Pollen consumption begins as early as two hours after the worker e-merges, reaches the maximum level in about five days, then diminishes by the tenth day. This corresponds with the time that she serves as a nurse bee. If she is "forced" to serve as a nurse for an extended period, pollen consumption will continue. During her lifetime the average honey bee worker will eat between 120 and 140 mg (0.042 and 0.049 oz) of pollen. During this period, internal bodily changes will take place also. The protein content of the body of a worker increases 60% to 70%—some-what less in drones, about 40%. Proteins can shift from one part of the body to another, depending on need. In young bees, the brood food glands in the head are highly developed; later in life as she secretes wax or begins to forage, glands or muscle tissues associated with these op-erations develop.

Pollen is a nutritious material rich in protein but, like many natural products, quite variable in composition. The crude protein varies from 8% to 40%, average 23%. Amino acid analysis of pollens indicates that they contain the essential amino acids in sufficient amounts for normal growth and development of the honey bee. Total protein in the honey bee diet needs to range between 23% and 30%. Honey bees maintained on a diet of less protein failed to rear brood. Because pollen is often in short supply, numerous studies have been devoted to better understanding the relationship of pollen to honey bee nutrition. Although fresh pollen is eaten, most of it is packed into cells where it undergoes lactic acid fermentation. This product is sometimes called bee bread. There is no difference in nutritive value between bee bread and fresh pollen, al-though the small quantity of starch (1% to 2%) disappears from bee bread. Pollen which is collected from returning foragers as they enter the hive and then immediately dried and stored at room temperature loses some of its quality in one year. If it is stored in a deep freezer, the pollen's nutritional qualities are retained for up to two years. Nutritional value or quality of pollen can be evaluated by chemical analysis or by feeding trials. Feeding trials can be performed by using a known quantity of workers and a laying queen in a small hive confined to a large ($3m^2 \times 2m$ high) screened cage free of flowering plants. After an adjustment period, known quantities of pollen (or any other protein food) in the form of a moist patty can be placed in each hive. Two criteria can be used to rate the food: its acceptability by weighing the quantity eaten, and its nutritional value as judged by the number of brood reared within a specific time period. The more brood reared, the better the quality of protein.

Under normal conditions, honey bees eat pollen obtained from a variety of plants. Experimentally, single source pollens were evaluated in feeding trials. Of the five tested, all met the minimal nutritional requirements of honey bees, but significant differences were noted. Sweet clover *(Melilotus sp.)* and black locust pollen *(Robinia pseudoacacia)* were more attractive than boxelder *(Acer negundo)*, willow *(Salix sp.)*, and blackberry *(Rubus allegheniensis)*. Boxelder and black locust pollen were more efficient in rearing brood than others. This was determined by the quantity of brood reared per gram of pollen consumed, and sweet clover produced the most bees during the test period. Mixed pollen, a combination of the five single sources under evaluation plus others from the area, ranked near the average of the five. In overall performance, the pollens were ranked, in descending order, sweet clover, black locust, mixed pollen, boxelder, willow, and blackberry (Campana 1975).

Some pollen grains are known to be tough. They resist degradation in concentrated acids, hot alkali, and grinding. It is believed generally that honey bees degrade them enzymatically in the digestive tract. While special enzymes are present in the honey bee's gut, it is unknown whether they originate in the honey bee, from the microflora in the gut, or are contained in the pollen grains. Pollens vary greatly in their nutritive value to honey bees as based on chemical analysis. Whether foragers selectively collect the best available, or gather whatever happens to be present, is unknown. It is possible to formulate a diet based on crude protein and essential amino acids from other food materials. No one has succeeded in blending one that is completely satisfactory for honey bees and equal to pollen in nutritive value.

FATS

Fat (lipid) requirements of honey bees are also supplied by pollen. There is some evidence to suggest that fat is stored in the body and can be used during periods of starvation and in normal growth and development. Especially in northern areas, "fall" bees have a higher total body fat then "spring" and "summer" bees. Fatty acids are necessary components of phospholipids which are an integral part of cellular structure and activity. The fatty acids are primarily of saturated long chain type—oleic, palmitic, and stearic, not closely correlated to what is found in pollen. Many insects cannot synthesize sterols so some type or types must be contained in the diet. Tissues of honey bees contain 24-meth-

TABLE 6.3. MINIMAL LEVELS OF AMINO ACIDS REQUIRED FOR OPTIMAL GROWTH OF HONEY BEES, AND AMINO ACID CONTENT OF SEVERAL PROTEINS (EXPRESSED AS % CRUDE PROTEIN)

Amino Acid	Minimal Level Required by Honey Bees	Royal Jelly	Pollen				Casein	Soybean Flour	Whole Egg Powder	Potato Flour
			Willow	Larkspur	Sweet Corn	Mixed				
arginine	3.0	5.1	5.6	4.4	4.7	5.7	3.4	7.7	6.2	4.9
histidine	1.5	2.2	2.0	3.5	1.5	2.4	2.7	2.3	2.4	1.4
lysine	3.0	6.7	5.9	6.3	5.7	6.4	6.9	6.6	7.5	5.3
tryptophane	1.0	1.3	1.5	1.4	1.6	1.3	1.2	1.5	1.5	1.0
phenylalanine	2.5	4.1	3.7	4.4	3.5	3.9	4.8	5.1	4.8	4.4
methionine	1.5	1.9	1.9	1.8	1.7	1.8	2.8	1.4	3.3	1.2
threonine	3.0	4.0	3.8	3.9	4.6	4.0	3.9	3.9	4.7	3.9
leucine	4.5	7.7	7.0	6.7	5.6	4.0	8.7	8.0	9.0	4.9
isoleucine	4.0	5.3	5.2	5.1	4.7	6.7	5.7	5.3	5.8	4.3
valine	4.0	6.7	6.0	6.0	6.0	5.7	6.6	5.3	6.8	5.3

Source: From Campana (1975), Harp (1978), and Weaver and Kuiken (1951).

ylene cholesterol, which is also found in pollen. Under experimental conditions, honey bees fed sugar, but deprived of fat and pollen, synthesized substantial quantities of fat which are stored in the head and abdomen. Beeswax, a complex mixture related to fats, consists of long chained hydrocarbons, monohydric alcohols, acids, and hydroxyacids, which are synthesized from carbohydrates; however, the exact mechanism by which this is done is unknown.

VITAMINS, WATER, AND MINERALS

Like all other animals, honey bees require vitamins, which must be in proper balance with other foods, especially proteins. Pollen is exceptionally high in the water soluble vitamins. While only proteins are needed for the brood food gland to properly grow and develop, vitamins are essential for rearing brood.

Honey bees obtain water on special collecting trips and from nectar. As in all living things, water serves as a general solvent for most organic materials and salts, and is needed for metabolism in the cells of the body. Water needs vary with the seasons of the year. In spring, when brood rearing is underway and low moisture honey is used as food, extra water is needed to dilute the honey. During winter in northern climates, water usage is minimal and unless the hive has adequate ventilation, the water which results from metabolizing honey could be detrimental to the colony.

Honey bees do not collect minerals separately, but bring them in with water, nectar, pollen, and honey dew. Analysis has shown that pollen and bee larvae contain up to 27 trace elements. Phosphorus and potassium are the most abundant mineral elements found, followed by calcium, magnesium, sodium, and iron. Experimentally, the addition of small quantities of sodium chloride to sugar syrup or honey reduced the honey bee's longevity. Honey dew, which normally contains an abundant supply of mineral salts, is detrimental to honey bees when they are confined to the hive for a long time because of cold weather.

Much has been learned about the nutritional requirements of the colony; however, there are still unanswered questions. Precise information is required in order to make sound management decisions, and as the need for food production increases, so is there the need to know more about colony nutrition.

BIBLIOGRAPHY

CAMPANA, B.J. 1975. Comparison of brood production efficiency and attractiveness of several pure plant pollen sources for honey bees. M.S. Thesis. University of Wisconsin, Madison.

DADD, R.H. 1973. Insect nutrition: Current developments and metabolic implications. Ann. Rev. Entomol. *18*, p. 381–420.

DeGROOT, A.P. 1953. Protein and amino acid requirements of the honey bee *(Apis mellifera)*. Physiol. Comp. et Oecolog *3* FASC 2 and 3, 90.

DIETZ, A. 1975. Nutrition of the adult honey bee. *In* The Hive and the Honey Bee. Edited and published by Dadant and Sons, Hamilton, Ill.

HARP, E.R. 1978. Potatoes: A pollen supplement for honey bees. Am. Bee J. *118* (3) 152-153.

HAYDAK, M.H. 1970. Honey bee nutrition. Ann. Rev. Entomol. *15*, p.143-156.

HERBERT, E.W., JR., H. SHIMANUKI, and D. CARON. 1977. Caged honey bees, comparative value of some proteins for initiating and maintaining brood rearing. Apidologie *8* (3) 229-235.

HERBERT, E.W., JR., H. SHIMANUKI, and D. CARON. 1977. Optimum protein levels required by honey bees to initiate and maintain brood rearing. Apidologie *8* (2) 141-146.

SHALLENBERGER, R.S., and G.G. BIRCH. 1975. Sugar Chemistry. AVI, Westport, Conn.

WEAVER, N., and K.A. KUIKEN. 1951. Quantitative analysis of the essential amino acids of royal jelly and some pollens. J. Econ. Entomol. *44* (5) 635-637.

7

The Business of Bees

This chapter is designed not to explain the details of keeping honey bees, but to describe some of the reasons why certain operations are performed. Suppliers of beekeeping equipment, packaged bee producers, and the U.S. Department of Agriculture through the Extension Service and some Land Grant State Universities publish excellent circulars and bulletins on how to assemble equipment, install honey bees, and other basic information. Equipment manufacturers and dealers are interested in beginners' success as their business depends on satisfied and successful beekeepers.

Honey bees can be kept anywhere flowering plants grow and where there is a suitable location for a hive. Other than in large downtown metropolitan areas, these conditions exist practically everywhere. The basic requirements of a colony are the same regardless of where it is kept. It needs food—nectar and pollen—and a place to establish a home, the hive. The management principles are quite similar whether the colony is managed as a business or as a hobby. In a business operation, the objective is to utilize labor and capital efficiently so as to obtain the highest possible return on investment; while as a hobby, bees are managed for the pleasure or challenge, profits are a secondary consideration.

All beekeeping enterprises can be grouped into one of three categories: full-time, part-time, or hobby. The majority of the *colonies* are managed by people in a full-time business operation, while the majority of the *individuals* engaged in beekeeping are classified as hobbyists. For convenience and for statistical purposes, those who have 10 or fewer colonies are considered hobbyists, 11 through 300 part-time, and over that, commercial or full-time. Some states, for tax and other regulatory purposes, classify individuals with 50 or more colonies as farmers. These figures are not absolute. One individual could manage fewer colonies intensively and derive an adequate income to give him the minimum standard of living, while someone else may have a relatively large number of colonies but managed less intensively and be considered a part-time beekeeper. Many people become involved in beekeeping as a hobby, either by self-study and/or enrolling in evening classes sponsored by local schools or beekeeping associations. Others learn the art or business through an informal apprenticeship within the immediate family, or by helping a beekeeper friend during the busy season, or by working as seasonal help for a large enterprise.

For someone interested but inexperienced in handling colonies the most logical way to begin is to purchase several hives and learn to manipulate and handle them on a small scale and then expand with experience. Managing colonies is different from working with domesticated animals. They learn to adjust and adapt to the owner and their immediate environment, while honey bees are wild animals which will not adjust to man's interest. Therefore, a beekeeper has to understand their basic biology and behavior and then make decisions accordingly.

KEEPING BEES IN SUBURBIA

Many suburban areas produce an abundance of nectar and pollen. However, there are other considerations. The mere presence of a hive in an adjoining or nearby lot will frighten many people, so prudent bee-keepers have learned to hide the hive behind a fence or shrubs. Some have located hives on top of a flat roof building out of public view. Keeping the hives inside a fenced area often is a necessary precaution so that small children wandering nearby are not stung. The hive should be situated so that the normal flight pattern is not over a busy street, sidewalk, or clothesline. In arid regions or during periods of drought, honey bees require water and will usually forage around swimming pools, bird baths, and drinking fountains. While providing a water source is no guarantee that honey bees will use it, this may reduce the tendency for them to pester neighbors. In most situations, honey bees foraging for water present no serious hazard, except around swimming pools where people often get stung when honey bees are stepped on or sat on.

Sometimes an innocent beekeeper can be falsely accused of creating a problem. The general public usually does not distinguish among wasps, hornets, yellow jackets, or honey bees which establish their colony in a hollow tree or wall of a building. Under these circumstances, a beekeeper may find it very difficult to prove that his bees are not involved in the problem.

Liability for bee stings is decided by the courts, but to establish who owns the honey bee which was responsible for a specific sting is extremely difficult or almost impossible, especially if the incident happened some distance from the hive. There is no way to prove, beyond a reasonable doubt, that the offending worker came from a specific hive. Honey bees also have been the subject of numerous court cases not only because of stings, but on ownership of swarms, trespassing, and when they are killed by insecticides. An extensive treatment of this subject has been summarized by Doutt (1959).

Because of an unfortunate or unfavorable incident involving honey bees, some municipalities specifically prohibit keeping a colony, either by ordinance or zoning. However, communities which do not have such regulations have a *common nuisance* ordinance and can force a metropolitan beekeeper to move or destroy his operation. Beekeepers, as a group, strongly oppose passage of laws which prohibit beekeeping, but most reasonable ones agree that an improperly located or neglected hive can be a nuisance to neighbors. When these situations arise, they have actively supported regulatory officials utilizing the common nuisance ordinance. Beekeepers also have been instrumental in helping communities draft regulations pertaining to keeping bees in metropolitan areas. One such ordinance was passed by the city of Tucson, Arizona, in 1961, and is sometimes referred to as model in dealing with the metropolitan honey bee controversy.

In summary, the ordinance states:

A. No person shall establish or maintain any hive, stand, or box where bees are kept, or keep any bees in or upon premises within the corporate limits of this City unless the bees are kept in accordance with the following provisions:

    1. If bee colonies are kept within fifty feet of any exterior boundary of the property on which the hive, stand, or box is located, a barrier that will prevent bees from flying through it, and not less than five feet high, shall be installed and maintained along said exterior boundary. Said barrier may be either a plant or be artificial.

    2. Fresh, clean watering facilities for bees shall be provided on the said premises.

    3. The bees and equipment shall be kept and maintained in accordance with the laws, rules, and regulations of the State.

B. Nothing in this section shall be deemed or construed to prohibit the keeping of bees in a hive, stand, or box located or kept within a school or university building for the purpose of study or observation.

KEEPING BEES IN RURAL AREAS

Locating several hives or establishing a beeyard in rural areas presents no serious problems. In northern areas successful beekeepers over the years have learned to place them next to buildings, hedges, or even along snow fences, where they are sheltered from the cold winter winds. The south edge of a forested area would be preferred over a deeply shaded site. An all-weather road should lead to the yard so that hives can be periodically inspected. In areas where the temperature is often above 32°C (90°F), placing hives so that they are in the afternoon shade is beneficial to the honey bees as well as to the beekeeper making routine inspections.

Grazing animals as a rule will not disturb hives, but will eat the grass around them. However, the hives should be situated so animals cannot walk between them, or far enough apart so a cow or a horse can turn around without bumping the hives. These animals will attempt to walk between hives; rather than back out or go straight forward, they usually try to turn and are known to upset hives. Hives located in remote areas are subject to vandalism and theft. No simple solution to these problems is available.

EQUIPMENT

Honey bees thrive in any suitable cavity; however, if they are to be managed to suit the interests or needs of mankind, then special equipment will be needed. Many states have laws which require honey bees to be kept in movable frames so that the bees can be inspected for diseases. In these states, regulatory agencies have the authority to destroy colonies kept in the historical skep, or any other makeshift containers. In years past, hives were designed to suit the interests and wishes of the beekeeper, rather than meet the needs or biological requirements of the honey bee. However, the discovery and patenting of *bee space* by Rev. L.L. Langstroth in 1851 made possible the development of a bee supply industry. While the size of hives has changed, the internal components are designed around his basic discovery. The hive still bears his name today.

Currently, equipment is a compromise between the needs of a honey bee and what a beekeeper can conveniently handle. The 10-frame hive body is considered standard, but some prefer to use an 11- or 12-frame hive body. Two standardized depths of hive bodies are used: 24.44 cm (9⅝ in.) and 16.8 cm (6⅝ in.). They usually are referred to as deep and shallow, respectively. Hive bodies designed for comb honey production are 14.44 cm (5 11/16 in.) or 12.22 cm (4 13/16 in.). Frames are standardized to fit the respective hive bodies.

Many beekeepers use 1, 2, or even 3 deep hive bodies as brood chambers and 2, 3 or 4 shallow ones for honey supers per colony. While shallow hive bodies are easier to manipulate when full of honey, they are usually more expensive on a per cubic foot of hive space. Some feel that shallow hive bodies used as supers hasten the honey ripening process. It is also easier to manipulate and manage the brood chamber as required for high honey

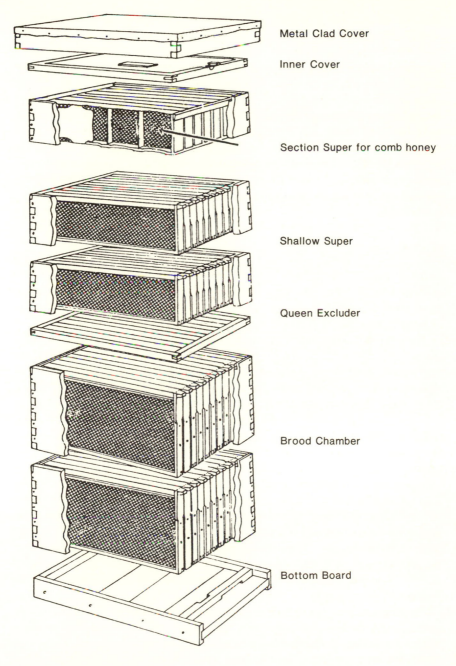

Metal Clad Cover

Inner Cover

Section Super for comb honey

Shallow Super

Queen Excluder

Brood Chamber

Bottom Board

FIG. 7.1. STANDARDIZED HIVE

Basic principles discovered by Langstroth in 1851 are in use today.

production when using shallow supers, and finally, all frames are interchangeable.

Woodworking enthusiasts can make their own components using plans obtained from the U.S. Department of Agriculture or by purchasing one unit and using it as a pattern. Nevertheless, it should be cut to exact specifications similar to factory-made equipment.

Pine is used to make the wooden parts of the hive. However, other kinds would also be satisfactory. Wood used for hive bodies should be such that it does not warp, or split easily. While light wood is preferred, it is not essential. The bottom boards should be made of decay-resistant wood such as cedar, redwood, or cypress, or it should be treated with a wood preservative. While some set their hives directly on the ground, others place them on concrete slabs, rocks or on old lumber to keep the bottom board off the ground.

Pressed wood, fiberboard, and plastic materials have, from time to time, appeared on the market, but have not been widely accepted because of cost.

FOUNDATIONS AND COMBS AND OTHER SUPPLIES

Two developments which occurred in the 19th Century made beekeeping possible as practiced today. The discovery of bee space was number one, and the making of comb foundations from beeswax was, undoubtedly, number two. Comb foundation is made by embossing a thin sheet of beeswax with the base and beginning of sidewalls of cell walls. It is attached to a frame and placed in the hive. The advantages of using a foundation on which workers build comb are two-fold. The comb is constructed straight, which simplifies manipulation of the frames and makes extraction of honey relatively simple. Foundation normally is embossed with worker-size cells. When workers are allowed to build natural comb without foundation, they build up to 25% drone cells, especially in early spring when nectar is abundant.

Three types of foundation are available. That which is used for brood and extracting comb is made of a deep yellow or somewhat darker wax and reinforced with spring steel crimped wires. Foundation designed to be used for comb honey is made of lighter colored wax and is thinner. Regular foundation runs about 16 sheets per 0.45 kg (per lb) of wax, while that used for comb honey averages between 20 and 25 sheets per 0.45 kg (per lb) of wax.

Plastic base comb foundation covered with a thin layer of beeswax is available. This foundation is more durable, does not need the reinforcing wires normally used to support wax foundation, and can be installed quickly into frames without fear of breakage. One disadvantage is that wax has a tendency to separate from the plastic base, and then bees refuse to build comb over that area.

Combs including frames made of plastic have appeared on the market. A suitable one would have some advantages. For example, frames of sealed honey could be placed in a high speed extractor without uncapping. Should the colony become infected with foulbrood, these combs could be easily sterilized and plastic comb would not be subject to wax moth damage. The products which have appeared on the market have had varying degrees of success. If honey bees are given a choice, such as placing five natural combs or five plastic ones in the same hive body, they prefer to use the natural ones over the synthetics; but if they have no choice, the plastic ones are accepted.

Smoker, bee veil, hive tool, and gloves also are considered essential pieces of equipment available from beekeeping equipment suppliers. While an extractor is an essential piece of equipment also, beginners have several options. In some areas, custom extraction is available. Some dealers also rent extractors, and several individuals can purchase a small extractor jointly, thus reducing expenses.

SMOKER

The smoker is an indispensable tool in beekeeping. Earliest use of smoke to pacify honey bees is not recorded; however, the smoker in use today is a device made by Moses Quinby in 1870. Smoke does three things to honey bees. (1) It tends to repel them; by judicious use workers can be driven downward or away from a specific area. (2) It stimulates some workers to engorge on honey, making them less defensive. (3) It dulls their senses, or masks odors. Disturbed, stinging and crushed honey bees emit an alarm pheromone which stimulates others to become highly defensive.

Smoke can be generated by slow-burning rotted wood, corn cobs, dried leaves, conifer needles, grass, or wood shavings. Rolled paper, rags, twine, and burlap are also suitable provided these materials are not treated or coated with an unknown or toxic material. Some safe materials may generate toxic gases when burned.

Careless use of smokers has started fires and even destroyed hives. While a smoker can be hazardous in some areas, it is essential if colonies are to be efficiently managed.

USED EQUIPMENT

There are times when used equipment becomes available for very good reasons. Caution should be exercised before buying or even receiving it free. Some states require an official inspection to insure it is disease-free before it can be moved from the premises or sold. Some states will not allow used equipment to be imported; others require an official health certificate from the state of origin. The reason for such regulations is simple and justified. The bacteria causing foulbrood remain on equipment for an extremely long time. Evidence of the disease is easily detected on old brood comb by knowledgeable beekeepers. Before purchasing, a beginner should become acquainted with laws. If there are no laws, it would be advisable to have an experienced beekeeper examine the brood comb to determine whether there is evidence of disease before the transaction is completed.

TO START

There are several ways to begin a beekeeping enterprise. The options are a personal choice and have no effect on the honey bees. Hobby kits that contain all the necessary items to begin are available or an individual can buy component parts separately. However, beginners should consider starting with at least two colonies, and possibly not over ten. The reason is simple: should the queen of this newly installed colony die before she lays eggs, the colony is hopelessly queenless and will eventually die. If there are two colonies and one queen dies, this queenless one can be combined with the *queen-right* colony. While both could die, the probability of this happening is much less.

The most popular way to begin an adventure with honey bees is to buy all the necessary components: queen, workers, and all the necessary hive parts and accessory equipment. Assembling the equipment, installing the packaged bees, and observing the colony grow provides an excellent opportunity for the individual to learn the basics of colony growth, development, and behavior. There are disadvantages: substantial amount of labor is required to assemble the equipment. There is a risk in installing the package of bees and releasing the queen, and the first year's honey crop is smaller than what could be expected from a full-sized hive.

It is also possible to buy the nucleus of a colony (nuc). While there is no standardized or legal definition of a nuc, it includes a laying queen and from three to five frames (combs) of brood and attached bees. These are transferred to the new owner's equipment. There is less risk starting with a nuc than with a package because the queen is laying. As a rule, a colony started from a nuc will produce more honey the first year than one from a package.

Purchasing a full-size colony is the third option. In addition to buying bees, a queen, and comb, other parts of the hive are included. The price will depend on supply and demand, and also on condition of the equipment such as decayed bottom board and damaged hive bodies. Although the beekeeping operation is under way immediately, the beginner has fewer opportunities to watch the orderly growth of the colony. Ownership can be transferred at a negotiated or mutually agreeable date, although it is easier to move the hive when the honey supply is low as it would be in spring or immediately after the honey is extracted.

Packaged bees should be ordered well in advance of the date they are to be installed. Industry has standardized 0.9- and 1.3-kg (2- and 3-lb) packages. The 1.3 kg (3-lb) package normally is used when the bees are installed on foundation, whereas a 0.9 kg (2-lb) package is suggested for installation on drawn comb. In either case, these bees will not be around during the nectar flow. Their value is in producing brood which will bring in nectar at a later date. Enough bees are contained in a 0.9 kg (2-lb) package to care for the brood produced by a normal queen, and the extra bees in a 1.3 kg (3-lb) package are useful in building comb.

A colony started from a package will reach full strength about 12 weeks after installation, and unfortunately in some areas this is after the peak nectar flow. However, if nectar is available over a long period, package bees can produce a reasonable crop of honey.

The ideal time to install package bees is a compromise. The earlier they are installed, the better are the possibilities of obtaining a larger honey crop. This is offset by the need to supplement their feed. Most people like to install packages as close to the early fruit bloom as possible, realizing that this is variable. It depends on climate, and beginners should have plans to supplementary feed newly installed packages.

One characteristic of our day and age is change—some critics say planned obsolescence. Beekeeping is unique. The basic equipment used in beekeeping has changed little since the mid-19th Century, and no change is anticipated in the future. It is possible that there will be innovations in mechanical handling of hives and honey, and there may even be new and different materials for hives and even combs. But the basic hive (a cavity) will remain the same. It hasn't changed dramatically since bees first evolved 150 million years ago.

BEEKEEPING RECORDS

Regardless of the size of a beekeeping enterprise, financial records are an important part of the operations. They must be complete and accurate if they are to be of value in making business management and income tax decisions. Some states specify the number of colonies a person must operate in order to be considered legally a farmer. Tax liability may vary depending on whether the operation is a hobby or business.

Cost of individual hive bodies, frames, and foundations can be accumulated and recorded as one hive body with combs. Depreciation should be reasonable, consistent, and accurate. While frames and combs may last indefinitely, many depreciate the hive body unit over a ten-year period. A prudent operator ought to consult with competent and knowledgeable tax authorities on the latest regulations and opinions.

· In addition to financial records, some beekeepers find biological data of interest and, often, of use. The date of first and major pollen flow, nectar flow, end of honey flow, and the onset of cold weather are important to know if colonies are to be managed for maximum profit.

BIBLIOGRAPHY

DADANT, C.C. 1975. Beekeeping equipment. *In* The Hive and the Honey Bee. Edited and published by Dadant and Sons, Hamilton, Ill.

DOUTT, R.L. 1959. The case of the trespassing bees. Bull. Entomol. Soc. Am. *5*(3) 93-97.

FARRAR, C.L. 1967. Life of the honey bee. Am. Bee J. *107*(12) 461-464.

GOJMERAC, W.L. 1978. Honey: Guidelines for efficient production. Univ. of Wisconsin Ext. Publ. A 2083. Madison.

JAYCOX, E.R. 1976. Beekeeping in the Midwest. Univ. of Illinois Circ. 1125. Urbana.

MORSE, R.A. 1975. Bees and Beekeeping. Comstock Publishing Associates, Cornell University Press, Ithaca, N.Y.

OWENS, C.D., and B.F. DETROY. 1969. Selecting and operating beekeeping equipment. U.S. Dep. Agric. Bull. *2204*.

ROOT, A.I., E.H. ROOT, H.H. ROOT, and J.A. ROOT. 1975. The ABC and XYZ of Bee Culture. 36th edition. A.I. Root Co., Medina, Ohio.

USDA. 1971. Beekeeping in the United States. U.S. Dep. Agric. Handb. 335.

8

Essential Operations

Beekeeping operations are synchronized with plant growth and development, which are regulated by factors such as day length, climate, and rainfall. For convenience, these activities are designated as seasonal, but fall operations in northern United States and southern Canada would be different than in Florida and southern California. So management activities are affected by two variables, season and climate. Climatic regions can be arbitrarily designated as: warm, where the average temperature does not go lower than 10°C (50°F); temperate, ranges between −4°and 7°C (25° and 45°F); and cold, lower than −6.7°C (20°F). Some operations are not applicable to warm regions, and questionable in a temperate region.

The beekeeper's fiscal year ends when the honey crop is removed; however, beekeeping should be viewed as a continuous operation. The hobbyist or part-time beekeeper in the cold region has two options after the honey harvest. Colonies can be (1) prepared for winter or (2) killed. If killed, then the equipment is stored, and package bees are installed the following spring. Some larger operations move south for the winter.

While killing colonies after the honey season appears brutal and perhaps uneconomical, a number of successful beekeepers have done this for many years. This technique reduces overwintering risks, and extra honey can be sold. Pollen and some honey are left in the combs, so packaged bees can be installed relatively early the following spring. While the quantity of honey produced per colony may not equal that of an overwintered colony, the operation is profitable because of lower costs.

Based on past experiences, the approximate date of the end of the honey flow is known; so about three weeks prior, the queen is either placed in a small cage in the hive or removed. This allows all brood to emerge, leaving clean comb. In past years, hydrogen cyanide was used to kill honey bees; however, changes in regulations make its use currently illegal.

WINTER PREPARATIONS

The extent to which colonies need special winter preparations depends on climatic regions—minimal in warm areas and a little more extensive in temperate zones. However, the kind of preparations given colonies in cold regions determines whether they survive through the winter.

Winter preparations should begin after the honey crop is removed. Some believe requeening is the first step in getting ready for next year. There are differences of opinion as to how long a queen should be retained. While she may live up to seven or eight years, some requeen annually, others requeen a portion of their colonies in fall, and the remainder, the following spring. Probably the least desirable procedure is to allow colonies to requeen themselves and not mark them. Queens live a shorter time in areas where there is an abundance of nectar and pollen, and colonies dramatically increase in size. Late summer and fall requeening has specific merits in cold regions. The young queen will lay at a faster rate than an old one, thus providing an abundance of "fall bees." Also, they can be purchased at a lower price than in the spring. However, the old queen is difficult to locate in a large colony, and should this newly requeened colony not make it through the winter, the newly purchased queen is also lost. But these are not very strong arguments against fall requeening.

Requeening with queen cells has recently been promoted as a simple, labor-saving technique. Rather than searching for and removing the old queen and slowly releasing a young one, a queen cell is introduced to the colony, and this automatically requeens it. When she emerges, she will kill the old one and take over the colony. Others have tried this technique, but were not happy with results as many queens died before emergence or were not successful in killing the old one. As with any new technique or procedure, some details are not completely understood.

Colony size is an important consideration for overwintering. It has been observed for many years that a large (strong) colony has a better chance of surviving the winter than a small (weak) one. While these are relative terms, a strong colony is one containing at least two standard hive bodies full of workers, brood, and a healthy queen.

Weak colonies either should be destroyed or combined or divided among several others. Some look at this operation as a loss; however, it is far better to incur this loss at this time of the year than in mid-winter. The probability of a small colony surviving the winter is much less than that of a large colony, and should it be lost, the honey it consumed to that date is also lost.

Uniting colonies will result in some fighting and loss of some workers, especially if nectar is not available. This can be prevented or reduced if both colonies are sprayed with a light sugar syrup made by dissolving one part sugar in one part water, by weight. Another procedure is to place a sheet of newspaper between the chambers of the colonies to be combined. In a day or two, workers chew away the paper and combine peacefully. At a later date the combs can be rearranged, placing brood in the lower chamber and honey above.

Small colonies also have been successfully overwintered on top of a full-size hive separated by a screened inner cover or with a specially made screen in place of the inner cover. Sometimes the small cluster above will unite with the large one below and appear as one large cluster. A small amount of radiated heat from below also helps to warm the top one. It is important to periodically examine the top one so that its honey supply is not exhausted.

TEMPERATURE AND SURVIVAL

In warm and temperate climates an ordinary hive in good condition provides adequate protection for the cluster during winter. In colder areas, some extra provisions are beneficial.

Extensive research has been devoted in trying to reduce winter losses which at one time were thought to be due exclusively to low temperatures. But we now know that there are many factors which affect winter survival. In some regions placing hives in areas sheltered from the cold winds, but exposed to the sun, is adequate. For many years hives were hauled into basements and cellars. Sometimes losses were more severe than if colonies were left outdoors, and other times, benefits were noted. We now know that a parasitic disease can be a contributing factor to high winter losses. Today there is a drug available to help reduce its severity (p. 138).

Many beekeepers felt that leaving the colony outdoors was the answer if the colony was given sufficient honey. However, with the increased value of honey, there are those who feel there is economic justification to re-evaluate the overwintering problem. For many years it was common practice to insulate or wrap hives left outdoors. Some went so far as to provide electric hive heaters. This practice was based on the theory that conserving heat would reduce honey consumption. Precise measurements at various places inside and around the cluster proved that this idea was not entirely true. Cluster temperature remains relatively constant even though the outside temperature changes dramatically. The vacant areas inside the hive are not heated, but correspond rather closely to outside temperatures.

Honey bees begin to cluster at about 14°C (57°F), and as the temperature decreases the cluster becomes more compact. The surface remains between 6° and 8°C (43° and 46°F) regardless of surrounding temperature. As the temperature increases to 7°C (45°F) it begins to expand. Sufficient heat is generated by honey metabolism to equal heat lost by radiation from the cluster surface. These basic findings explain why a large cluster is better able to survive low temperatures than a small one. A small cluster loses more heat in proportion to a large one, because it has a greater surface area in relation to the cluster size. This also explains why heavy insulation does not reduce honey consumption as much as would be expected. In fact, insulation could be detrimental. While it will prevent rapid cooling of the hive interior, it also slows the late winter and early spring warm-up, which is beneficial to colony survival. On warm, sunny winter days, inside temperatures will increase to where the cluster can expand so some workers can take a "cleansing" flight or at least move to a new supply of honey in nearby cells. It is well known that extremely low temperature presents no unusual challenge to the well-prepared colony. They have been held in a freezer at −45°C (−50°F) for several months, and survived, provided honey was available. Colonies housed

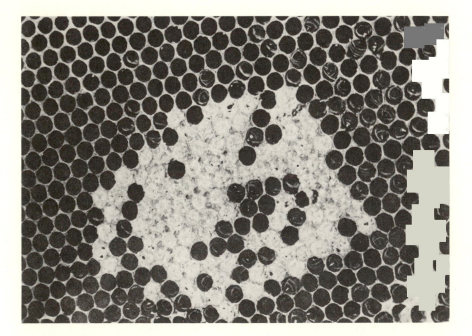

FIG. 8.1. WORKERS AND SEALED BROOD KILLED BY STARVATION AND LOW TEMPERATURE

Starving workers tend to crawl into cells prior to death.

in hives with portions of the sides removed, survived, if sheltered from wind. Prolonged low temperatures can present problems to a small cluster. It loses more heat proportionately and covers less honey than a large one. If it cannot move to a new supply, it will starve. The old adage "honey bees never freeze, but starve" appears to be true. More information on temperature regulation is on p. 36.

SUPPLEMENTARY FEEDING

It is argued that if a colony is handled properly there should be no reason for supplementary feeding. However, management involves more than allowing nature to take its course and collecting the surplus. Utilizing capital and labor, management employs the latest technology to achieve maximum benefits or profit. Ideally, at honey harvest time, enough honey should be left in the hive to carry the colony through the winter. Some years additional nectar is produced by late blooming plants; but if the hive is reduced to overwintering size, workers would not be able to gather it and some honey production is lost. Because of the many variables affecting nectar production, there is no way to predict whether late fall nectar will be available. Therefore, many prudent managers remove honey with the idea that they may have to feed some sugar at a later date. At one time, there were differences of opinion as to the benefits and hazards of feeding sugar to honey bees. Currently all evidence indicates that they can utilize sucrose as their only source of energy (p. 59).

The simplest way to feed sugar to a colony in warm and temperate areas is to give then dry granular sugar. It is ingested, converted to honey, and stored in combs. Water is brought in by foragers. The sugar must be placed in some type of container or receptical over the top bars or on the bottom board with the entrance closed. There are two disadvantages of feeding dry sugar. It is converted to honey quite slowly and it is difficult or impossible to add medications. While the rate at which it is converted to honey is not critical in warm regions, in cold areas it is important to have the colony fed before cold weather arrives.

Sugar "boards" were popular ways to feed colonies at one time. They are made by preparing a concentrated sugar solution boiled to the soft candy stage, then cast into a mold about 3.81 cm (1 ½ in.) thick and in any convenient dimensions to fit over the top bars of a standard hive body. Workers will cluster around this sugar board and slowly "eat" away at it. Considerable heat is required to prepare them and certain medications cannot be blended in the hot sugar syrup. But no special containers are required to handle or feed them.

A popular way to supplementary feed a colony is by preparing a heavy syrup from sugar. This is done by dissolving two parts sugar in one part water by weight. Some heat must be applied to completely dissolve the sugar. Medications can be mixed in the syrup when it cools. The two to one mixture is ideal for fall feeding, if it is more concentrated; some recrystallization occurs when it cools. If it is more dilute, the workers will have to evaporate the excess moisture, thus expending energy needlessly.

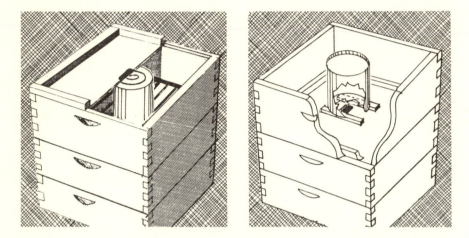

FIG. 8.2. *(LEFT)* FRICTION-TOP CONTAINER USED TO FEED HONEY BEES. SEVERAL CONTAINERS CAN BE PLACED DIRECTLY ON FRAMES FOR FALL FEEDING. *(RIGHT)* PLACING CONTAINERS ABOVE INNER COVER PREVENTS WORKERS FROM BUILD-ING COMB IN VACANT SPACE AROUND CONTAINER

There are a number of different ways to feed a colony sugar syrup. The friction top container such as a used coffee can, with several small holes drilled in the cover and inverted over the top bars or inner cover works well and is economical. Division board and entrance feeders are available from equipment suppliers. Various devices and containers and even plastic bags in which a standard frame can be inserted have been successfully used. Open top containers should have a float or some type of screen which prevents workers from falling or being pushed into the syrup and drowning. These feeders can be placed in an empty hive body or super above the inner cover, then covered with a top cover so the feeding devices are inside the hive being fed. Entrance feeders are convenient to use because the hive does not have to be opened before feeding; however, in cold weather, honey bees will not use them. Sugar syrup can be warmed before feeding, if required, especially when fed from a friction top container above the cluster.

While it is possible to feed sugar syrup from a community container outdoors, this practice has several disadvantages. It has a tendency to stimulate robbing, neighboring colonies could help themselves, and other insects such as ants and wasps also become a nuisance.

The amount of honey needed in a colony to assure its survival through winter is determined by geographic location. In cold areas it should have between 27.18 and 40.77 kg (60 and 90 lb), 13.59 and 27.18 kg (30 and 60 lb) in temperate regions, and 6.79 and 13.59 kg (15 and 30 lb) in warm zones. Some commercial operations routinely weigh all colonies in fall. Those lighter than their established minimum weight are fed a specific quantity of sugar syrup. The standard two to one sugar syrup mixture will add 3.171 kg (7 lb) to the colony for every 3.785 liters (4 quarts). Using this procedure an inexperienced crew can rapidly feed colonies for winter.

Some beekeepers prefer to feed extra sugar syrup in fall which reduces the possibility of having to feed in the late winter or early spring. Honey bees are unique creatures. They eat only what is needed and store the rest, but if a colony is as short as much as 0.227 kg (½ lb) it will starve.

ORGANIZATION WITHIN THE HIVE

Hive organization is also important to winter survival. Normally the queen begins laying eggs in the center of the cluster, in the form of a sphere, located towards the center of the hive, working slowly upward. Pollen is deposited in concentric layers to the sides and above, and honey to the outside of it. During normal hive manipulations in summer, the natural and ideal arrangement is sometimes upset. Unsealed honey, but not pollen, is readily moved if it is below the brood area. As fall approaches, sometimes the brood area will be in the second and third chamber and the lower or bottom one empty, or containing only pollen. The brood area should be lowered by removing the empty chamber. It can be placed in storage or set on top of the cluster if necessary. But it is very important that this new upper chamber not remain empty. If the cluster moves upward into the empty top chamber during cold weather, it will starve, even though honey is available at a lower level.

Ventilation is also important. For every 4.53 kg (10 lb) of honey about 3.785 liter (1 gal.) of water is released into the surrounding environment. During other times of the year this presents no unusual problem, but in winter moisture will condense and freeze on the cold surface, usually above the cluster. As temperatures moderate, this frost melts and drips on the cluster. While a strong cluster can usually take care of such problems, this can be harmful to a weak one. For many years there were strong differences of opinion as to the best remedy for this problem.

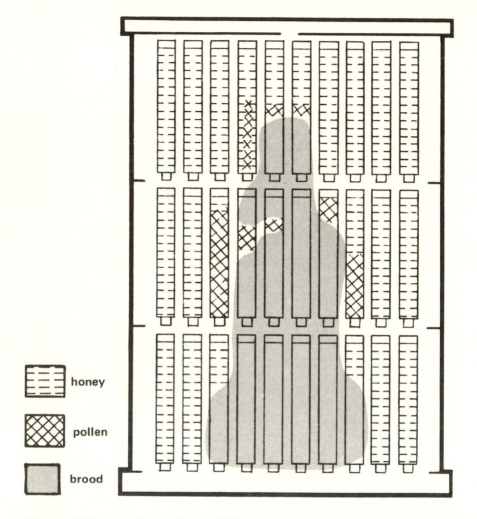

honey

pollen

brood

FIG. 8.3. IDEAL LATE FALL ARRANGEMENT; POLLEN AND HONEY ABOVE AND TO SIDES OF BROOD

Packing the area above the inner cover with absorbant or insulating material was one solution, another was heavy insulation, and a third was to simply drill a 2.54 cm (1 in.) hole in the top hive body. Those who believed in the conservation of heat theory, previously mentioned, argued that heat along with the moisture escapes the hive, and thus the colony uses significantly more honey. But by a series of precise temperature measurements this theory was proven to be incorrect, and currently an opening in the upper brood chamber is highly recommended for ventilation.

CONTROLLED ENVIRONMENT

Winter losses are costly and considerable effort is devoted to finding ways to reduce them. In years past, those who were able to or had facilities, moved colonies into buildings, basements, or cellars. There were strong differences of opinion as to the merits of this procedure. As labor became more expensive, but honey and energy cheap, the trend was toward outdoor wintering or moving to warmer regions. However, due to economic changes there is a renewed interest in overwintering in cold climates, but in controlled environment. Because more is known about colony requirements and some rather sophisticated temperature control equipment is available, significant progress has been made in holding colonies through winter on small quantities of honey. Temperature of the room or building must be maintained between 5.6° and 8.9°C (42° and 48°F).

Excess moisture can be removed by air circulation if some fresh air is drawn from outdoors. The building or room must be kept dark so entrance must be through double light-proof doors. Inspections, if required, should be made with a dim red light. Both heating and cooling equipment must be available, as a sudden warm day in January or February can be disastrous. Workers become activated, and many will leave the hive, get lost, and die.

Small colonies have been held in this type of environment for 15 weeks, consuming about 6.79 kg (15 lb) of honey. Colonies this size would not have survived outdoors in a cold region. While much is still to be learned, these results appear very encouraging. Overwintering in controlled environments may not be practical for the hobbyist; however, others will find the technique useful. As with any business, options chosen will depend on resources and interests of the operator. Extra queens might be purchased or raised in late summer. At the end of the nectar flow, full size colonies might be subdivided into small units, each with a young queen. They would be fed medicated sugar syrup and remain outdoors until cold weather arrived, then moved indoors. In spring, they would be moved outdoors and handled as newly installed packages or nucs.

WINTER OPERATIONS

Winter activities associated with beekeeping depend on climatic regions. In warm areas, queen and package producers and local crop pollinators usually are involved with this highly specialized operation. However, in cold regions, even if colonies were well prepared, a winter inspection is very important. They can be safely inspected at moderate temperatures, −6.7°C (20°F), if care is used. The covers should be removed gently so that the cluster is disturbed as little as possible. The only purpose for this inspection is to insure that the cluster is near a supply of honey. If it is in the lower chamber, with honey above, the colony is in excellent condition. However, if the cluster is relatively small and in the upper chambers, then frames on each side should contain honey. Empty ones should be exchanged with full ones. Sometimes switching frames within the same chamber is all that is necessary. Many colonies are lost by starvation every year in cold regions because this simple operation is not performed. Comb rearrangement is less critical towards spring and in temperate regions. Workers will readily move honey to where it is needed anytime the inside hive temperature is above 14°C (57°F).

In cold regions in late winter and early spring on warm sunny days, it is not unusual to notice considerable activity around colonies. Not only will workers carry out dead honey bees, but many will fly out and die, making a rather dramatic sight, especially if the area is covered with snow. Those flying out are the old ones, and others are taking a cleansing flight usually staining the snow. Staining will be more intense if the colony has a severe infection of nosema or was wintered on dark honey. Dead and dying bees outside the hive at this time of the year indicate that the colony is active and vigorous. In temperate and warm regions these same activities take place, but are not as conspicuous because of the absence of snow cover or lack of a prolonged cold period when dead and old bees have a tendency to accumulate in the hive.

Late Winter and Early Spring Activities

Regardless of outdoor temperatures, as days lengthen the queen begins to lay eggs at a rate dependent upon: (1) her genetic capability, (2) available pollen, (3) size of the cluster, and (4) space in the hive.

The supply of honey at this time is very critical. Honey utilization is rather modest during late fall and early winter because the colony is in a "dormant" period in the sense that cluster temperature is somewhat reduced because it is broodless. But with the initiation of brood rearing, honey consumption dramatically increases not only because of elevated temperature, but because it is used to feed larvae. Most winter losses occur at this time because of starvation *after* they survived the coldest part of the year, and it is usually the stronger colonies which die primarily because of the large amount of brood rearing.

The purpose of early spring inspection is to insure that the hive contains sufficient honey. Because of moderating temperatures at this time, the position of the honey is less critical as workers readily move it to where it is needed. Some successful beekeepers routinely feed colonies medicated light sugar syrup with the belief that the extra water can be used to dilute honey stored in combs, especially if the weather is such that workers cannot forage for winter.

IMPORTANCE OF PROTEIN

The size of the overwintered colony will be directly related to the amount of pollen gathered the previous season and will vary considerably between colonies within the same yard. Generally, those colonies which became queenless, or whose queen was superceded during the heavy pollen flow, will have more pollen because it was collected but not used. Frames containing pollen should be redistributed or equalized between colonies.

In warm and temperate areas some fresh pollen may be available as early as mid to late January and by mid to late March in cold regions. However, pollen stored in the combs is especially important because inclement weather usually does not allow for continuous collection. While a colony can rear brood for about two weeks without pollen, interrupted brood rearing is detrimental to the colony's growth and surviving workers.

In cold regions at this time, pollen must be within the cluster to be of value, as it is eaten directly from cells. As weather moderates workers will travel throughout the hive to find and eat it, but by this time these colonies may be retarded in growth.

Colony development proceeds at a predictable rate if all its needs are met. Observations and experiments over many years indicate that if adequate pollen is available about eight weeks before fresh pollen is produced, the colony will develop a large population and be able to capitalize on the first available fresh pollen and continue uninterrupted growth. On the other hand, colonies lacking pollen during this critical period undergo periods of very little or no brood production, and when natural pollen finally is available, this small colony is not able to fully exploit the situation. The importance of a large colony, whether it is for pollination, honey production, or producing packaged bees for sale cannot be overemphasized.

Beekeepers and some writers tend to use the terms honey flow and nectar flow interchangeably, but there is an important distinction. Nectar flow refers to the capacity of plants to produce nectar which is influenced by such factors as plant species, soil type, fertility, moisture, temperature, and hours of sunshine. Honey flow refers to the relationship between the colony and available nectar supply. Factors such as colony size, brood rearing, hive space organization, and temperature influence honey flow. Honey flow may vary greatly between colonies exposed to the same nectar flow.

A good queen will lay about 1,600 eggs per day. It takes 21 days for brood to complete development and the average worker lives about 5 to 6 weeks. The ratio between brood and population decreases 10 to 14% for each increase of 10,000 workers, whereas the average daily rate of egg laying by the queen increases with a rise in population up to 40,000 bees (Farrar 1968). A large colony produces more brood than a small one, and at the same time has a larger percentage of workers available for gathering nectar and pollen when it is available. A large colony will produce more honey, gather more pollen, or be more effective in pollination, not only because of sheer numbers, but a small colony needs most of its workers to rear brood.

Because of the importance of pollen to the welfare of a colony, many other sources of proteins have been evaluated with the hope of finding a pollen substitute. While much has been learned about the honey bee's nutrition, no one has succeeded in blending a completely satisfactory substitute. Many well-known proteins appear to contain all the essential amino acids; however, either the workers refuse to eat it, or brood rearing ceases when the material is consumed. A colony fed a substitute should continue brood rearing indefinitely. Among the items evaluated were dried egg yolk, expellar process soybean flour, dried brewers and bakers yeast, dried skim milk, casein, meat scraps, other yeasts, boiled potatoes, and possibly others not reported. That honey bees cannot detect nutritional value of a food is not unusual; however, some believe pollen contains an unknown feeding stimulant, because many well-known protein sources are not consumed unless some pollen is blended into it. Other substances might be consumed when blended with sugar or honey but brood rearing either decreases or stops. While some commercially available materials are called pollen substitutes they actually are extenders or supplements.

A satisfactory supplement can be made by extending 0.454 kg (1 lb) of pollen with 1.36 kg (3 lb) of expellar process soy flour or brewers yeast (see pollen trapping, p. 99). Either of the two dry ingredients plus pollen is mixed with a heavy sugar syrup and formed into a moist patty and placed over the top bars immediately above the cluster. Supplementary feeding should begin about six to eight weeks before natural fresh pollen is available. The colony should have a continuous supply of this mixture until fresh pollen is regularly available, and at that time they will not eat the supplement. The average colony will use about 0.454 kg (1 lb) of this mix per week. The one to three mixture will sustain brood rearing indefinitely. Trapped pollen is not readily or always available, but feed-

FIG. 8.4. FEEDING POLLEN SUPPLEMENT OR SUBSTITUTE

ing either brewers yeast or expellar process soy flour mixed with heavy sugar syrup without pollen is beneficial. Workers will eat it and continue brood rearing provided some pollen is available in the hive or foragers can fly out and gather small quantities of it outdoors on warm days.

REVERSING CHAMBERS

Most colonies are overwintered in two or three hive bodies, and by spring the brood normally will be in the upper part of the hive. With the availability of fresh pollen and nectar, the queen increases her rate of egg laying and space becomes the limiting factor affecting colony growth. The normal behavior of the colony is to expand upward in the hive. Extra pollen and nectar are stored above and to the sides of the brood area. During periods of heavy production, they are stored in any available space including empty cells within the brood area. This either slows the queen's rate of egg laying, or the colony begins to prepare for swarming. While some beekeepers close the top auger hole forcing the workers to use the lower entrance, the behavior of the queen and cluster are not greatly affected, as she will not move to the lower chamber. Reversing brood chambers has been a long established practice by which the queen is lowered. This is done by tipping the hive to one side or back, and then placing what was the top chamber next to the bottom board, and the empty bottom chamber on top. Workers and the queen will not abandon the brood in lowered chamber, and space above is now available. If this is done before a nectar flow, some frames containing honey should be placed in the top chamber.

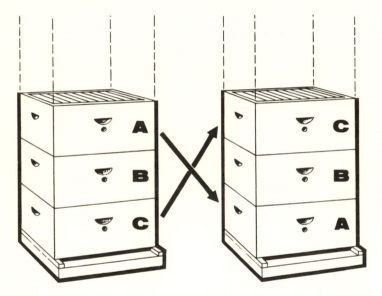

FIG. 8.5. REVERSING BROOD CHAMBERS "AROUND THE MIDDLE"

DIVIDING

Some argue against building large colonies early in the season, as later on more time must be spent on swarm control, especially if the colony contains an old queen. Swarming tendency can be reduced by removing some workers which could be sold as packaged bees, or by dividing the colony. In warm areas a colony can be divided practically anytime; however, in temperate and cold regions the time to divide is at least eight weeks before the beginning of the major nectar flow. Extra queens should be available. The hive is dismantled and the queen is located. She is placed in one chamber, preferably the lower one, along with about half of the brood and attached bees. This chamber is now completely covered with a piece of plywood, or many beekeepers simply use the inner cover with the center hole blocked. The other hive body which contains the remainder of the workers and brood is placed above the covered lower chamber. The critical step is to make certain that there is a complete separation between the upper and lower chamber, and each one should have its own supply of honey, pollen, and separate entrances. The new queen can now be introduced into the queenless upper chamber by the slow release method. While there are several ways to slow release a queen, perhaps the simplest technique is to use the queen shipping cage. Remove the end cork and puncture a small hole with a sharp object or nail in the candy plug which served as food during shipping. The queen cage should be placed between frames with the candy plug upwards, to prevent any worker accompanying the queen from blocking the escape hole should she die before being released. Workers will be immediately attracted to a new queen and will eat the candy plug which keeps her in the cage. In two or three days she will be released and begin to lay eggs. The slow release method is necessary so that the colony has a chance to adjust to its new queen.

In several days the colony should be inspected to see if the queen has been released. If not, the wire screen can be removed from the cage and the queen allowed to move among the workers. This one large colony now has been divided into two separate colonies, one on top of the other. After one or two weeks, the top colony can be moved to its separate location or the divided colony can be operated as a two-queen colony.

Using the same basic procedure, two independent colonies can be formed immediately from one large one. An extra top cover and bottom board, in addition to the queen, are required. The old queen and about half of the brood and attached workers are moved to the new location several feet from the site of the original colony. The new queen is introduced to the remaining half of the colony on the old site. Workers will not abandon their queen at the new site, and returning field workers will return to the old site and readily accept their new queen after she is released.

Sometimes it is rather difficult to find the queen in an established colony, or commercial beekeepers hesitate to spend time searching. About three or four days before the date of division, the colonies are separated as previously described without regard to location of the queen. On the day the queen is introduced, the colony is examined for the presence of eggs. By this time, all eggs laid by the old queen would have hatched, so the new queen is introduced into that portion which is without eggs. It is assumed that the old queen is in the other portion of the hive. If the queenless portion, by chance, had eggs on the date it was divided, the colony would have begun to raise its own, as detected by the presence of developing queen cells. These must be destroyed, as such a colony will not accept an introduced queen. Another reason for non-acceptance is the mother-daughter queen combination. The mother may be marked so she is removed, but the daughter is overlooked. Attempting to introduce a new queen to such a colony also will result in failures. Professional beekeepers expect failures in about ten percent of the colonies requeened, so will buy extra ones.

Allowing a divided colony to requeen itself naturally is possible in warm regions. Although a new queen is produced in two weeks, it will be about three weeks before she is laying eggs. A three-week delay in brood production before the honey season will undoubtedly result in a substantial reduction in honey crop for that year. In many areas, the weather is unpredictable in spring which could result in queens' failure to mate which results in drone layers.

After the new colonies are adjusted to their new status, they can be balanced by moving frames of sealed brood from the stronger to weaker ones. As workers emerge, they will stay with the colony into which they were born.

MANIPULATIONS DURING THE HONEY FLOW

Many older books on beekeeping placed considerable emphasis on capturing and placing swarms in hives. At one time, this was the way beekeepers increased the size of their operation. While it is important to understand the basic principles of swarming (p. 48), with proper management swarming seldom should occur or take place in specific colonies such as those containing an old queen, and these should be inspected more frequently when possible.

Assume that on a specific day the queen is laying eggs in the lower brood chamber. In about two or three weeks she will have expanded her brood area into the second or third chamber, with honey and pollen stored to the sides and above. To avoid congestion, another chamber will have to be added, if there is a nectar flow underway and swarming is to be avoided. In the meantime, adult workers will be emerging from cells in the lower chambers. The queen will continue to move upward even into the honey super unless a queen excluder is placed over the brood chamber. The queen excluder is a grid with openings 4.14 mm (0.163 in.) formed by firmly attaching wires to a frame, or by punching oblong holes in a flat metal sheet. Workers can pass through the openings, but not the queen or drones. While this device keeps her out of the honey super, she will not move to the lower hive body on her own. Reversing brood chambers as previously explained puts her and the recently laid eggs and young larvae in the lower chamber where she will continue to lay. The lower chamber with its frames of empty cells and emerging workers will be reused. Reversing also moves young workers downward where they will feed developing larvae, thus relieving congestion near the top of the hive.

The frequency and time to reverse will be dependent on nectar flow and capacity of the queen to lay. The decision to reverse should be based on colony condition rather than on the calendar. Switching chambers should be done when the upper chamber contains eggs and young larvae, and the lowest chamber has either mature or emerging brood. The reversal operation can be done quickly. The colony is smoked, opened, and several frames in the top chamber inspected. If eggs and larvae are present, the colony is tipped back and brood chambers separated. Queen cup cells built on the lower edges of the frames are examined. If any contain an egg or developing larva, they should be destroyed and all other frames examined closely, as the colony was in an early stage of swarm preparation. The colony is reassembled placing the chamber which contains eggs and larvae next to the bottom board. This chamber normally will be the heaviest, as it also will contain some honey. Overlooked swarm cells will continue to develop even though the chambers were reversed. During peak brood rearing, the chambers may have to be reversed every 10- to 14-day period. Timely reversals greatly reduce the tendency to swarm and keep the queen out of the honey super.

If, on routine inspection, eggs are not present, there is a possibility that the colony is queenless, and queen cells in varying stages of development will be present. While the colony naturally requeens itself, about three weeks of brood production will be lost, substantially reducing the potential honey crop especially if the colony became queenless early in the season. Many beekeepers will maintain several (up to ten percent) queen nucs for such situations. Extra queens are kept in small (three- or four-frame), specially constructed hive bodies with a small population of workers. When a queenless colony is encountered, several empty frames are removed and replaced with those from a queen nuc. The queenless colony at this time quite readily accepts a new laying queen, especially if she is accompanied by some brood and workers; however, developing queen cells must be destroyed.

If, on routine inspection, the colony is congested with workers, nectar, and pollen, and swarm cells are in varying degrees of development, the colony is about to swarm. Swarming means not only a loss of workers, but a drastic reduction in honey production, so it should be prevented whenever possible. It is best to avoid conditions and combinations of circumstances which induce swarming, as it is easier to prevent than stop once the process is underway. As mentioned earlier, dividing a strong overwintered colony or removing workers which can be used or sold as packaged bees reduces the tendency to swarm.

It is possible to interrupt swarming by manipulating and "unbalancing" the colony. The queen, with several frames of eggs and young brood (if available) and some empty combs, should be confined to the lower brood chamber with a queen excluder. An empty hive body is placed immediately above the queen excluder, then the remaining brood is placed above the empty chamber. This arrangement upsets colony organization, at least temporarily, and in a week the queen excluder can be removed and the colony should return to normal.

There are differences of opinion on the use of a queen excluder to keep her confined to the brood area. Some maintain that forcing workers to crawl through it reduces the efficiency of the colony and honey production declines. "A queen excluder is also a honey excluder" is an old and frequent comment. While it is not a disaster to have the queen enter the honey super, it does create some extra work and inconvenience. Timely reversal of the brood chamber automatically keeps the queen there, and the reason she moved to the honey super is crowding. However, during a light honey flow workers will fill the brood chamber with honey and pollen, and it is only with reluctance that workers move through an excluder.

Keeping a partly filled or empty super immediately above the queen excluder helps stimulate workers to move upward. Adding empty supers above the brood area and moving the full but unsealed ones higher is referred to as bottom supering.

Colony inspection and manipulations should be done at regular intervals to provide or readjust space to provide for uninterrupted and unrestricted brood rearing and adequate space for honey storage. The frequency of inspection will depend, to a degree, upon the size of the operation. While the hobbyist may see fit to inspect and possibly rearrange some frames or hive bodies on a weekly basis, the part-time or commercial operator has to balance inspection labor costs with anticipated income derived from honey, and decide if more frequent inspections are justified. Timely inspections will quickly locate queenless colonies and overcrowding, which is conducive to swarming.

As in many businesses, the frequency of inspection is a compromise between what is best and what is practical. Maintaining a precise schedule is difficult because weather will not always allow inspections and manipulations. Keeping a colony on a scale and periodically recording weight changes is helpful. For example, if there is little or no weight change during a specific period, there is less urgency to inspect colonies than if there was a rapid gain in weight. The basic purpose of late spring and early summer inspections is to make certain that the colony has adequate space and that it does not swarm.

HONEY REMOVAL

Once combs are full and at least 75% of the cells are sealed, the honey can be extracted with some assurance that it will meet the required standard of identity. Some advocate that sealed combs be removed as soon as possible, so honey will not absorb objectionable or foreign odors from within the hive. Frequency of removal will depend on a variety of circumstances. If the honey flow is long, extracted combs can be returned immediately for refilling. These "wet supers" should be placed above a queen excluder or on top of several unsealed or partly filled ones. They are highly attractive to workers and are immediately cleaned, but if the queen is in the immediate vicinity she will go into them and begin laying eggs.

Many commercial operators delay extraction until all supers are "in from the field"; therefore, supers and combs are used only once per season. Labor costs associated with extraction are reduced, but investment in equipment is higher. It is possible to segregate supers that contain specific types of honey. In some areas, light colored or specific kinds (basswood, orange blossom) command a premium price and are extracted separately.

Dripping honey can be reduced if one or several days prior to removing supers all are pried loose and rotated 180°. Honey stored in bridge and brace comb is cleaned up by workers inside the hive, reducing the possibility of robbing. Workers can be removed from supers by a variety of methods. The hobbyist might simply remove individual frames and brush off the attached workers, while larger operators might use chemical repellents, a bee escape, or a stream of air. The brush should be soft bristled so the caps are not broken and fewer workers are injured.

Chemical repellents have been used to successfully drive workers out of supers. They work well for experienced operators, and those who are accustomed to paying close attention to details. A small quantity is placed on an absorbent pad above full supers inside an empty, shallow hive body. Vapors, along with a little smoke, drive workers downward, clearing the super. High concentrations tend to stupify, rather than repel. Temperature also is important to their performance. Propionic anhydride and glacial acetic acid work best when temperatures are above 26°C (80°F), while benzaldehyde works best below 26°C.

The bee escape is a mechanical device designed to fit in the center hole of the standard inner cover. By an arrangement of delicate springs, workers are permitted to pass only in one direction—out. An inner cover or a piece of plywood of similar size is sometimes referred to as escape board. Most of the workers will leave the super in a day or two after it is inserted below supers to be removed. Equipment above the supers evacuated of honey bees must be tight, otherwise workers from other hives will begin robbing the unprotected supply of honey. Care also must be exercised during warm weather. Wax combs might disintegrate because workers are not present to keep them cool.

Perhaps the simplest mechanical device to remove workers is an air stream. A blower delivering about 42.47 m³ (1500 ft³) per minute through a nozzle is an easy and rapid way of clearing a super. The hive body is tipped on end and the air stream is directed at the workers between the combs. Equipment suppliers have a number of different kinds of portable units, and it is also possible to make one using a power supply and a standard shop vacuum cleaner with a few adjustments and alterations.

Full supers should always be covered and hauled in a closed vehicle, not only to keep out dust, but so that workers don't begin robbing. Mechanical devices to lift and transport hives and supers are available from suppliers. While they are a necessity for the part-time and full-time beekeeper, some of them are optional for the hobbyist.

EXTRACTION AND PACKING HONEY

While the home kitchen may serve as an adequate and convenient place in which to handle honey for the hobbyist with several hives, commercial operations require more elaborate facilities. If honey is to be sold as a food for human consumption, some states have health and safety regulations governing the design, construction, and operation of such facilities. Regardless of the size of the operation, all honey handling installations should have an area or room in which to hold full supers, a place for uncapping combs, a location for the extractor, and a storage or bottling area for the final product. Devices to move supers and transfer honey such as hand trucks, pallets, fork lifts, pipes, and pumps will vary with the size and design of the operation.

In regions where honey is extracted in late fall, a room capable of being heated to about 32°C (90°F) is needed to warm the honey in combs making extraction easier. It is also possible to lower the moisture of uncapped honey in supers when necessary, by using a series of fans or a dehumidifier to remove excess moisture from the room. Supers have to be stacked to permit free movement of air.

Hand-operated, heated knives and partially automated uncapping machines have been developed to simplify and increase the efficiency of this operation. The method for handling wax cappings with associated honey is described on p. 114.

The basic principle of the extractor has changed little since 1865 when Major F. Hruska, in Austria, discovered that honey could be removed from combs by centrifugal force. Extractors available from suppliers range from simple two-frame, hand-operated types to radial ones designed to hold 72 frames with precise electrical controls. From large extractors, honey is transferred to a heated, 37° to 49°C (100° to 120°F), sump tank by gravity, so wax and other extraneous matter float to the surface, where they can be removed by screens or a series of baffles. Separating the extraneous material as soon as possible and at a low temperature reduces the possibilities of honey absorbing foreign odors or flavors.

After extraction, four options are open to the beekeeper depending on size of operation, investment in capital equipment, and whether honey is to be sold bulk or in retail containers. The honey is heated to:

(1) 49°C (120°F) then allowed to cool. Temperature control is important, but duration of the heating period is immaterial. Honey is placed in 27-kg (60-lb) containers or 209-liter (55-gal.) drums. No artificial cooling is necessary. This system is used generally by those who market their honey bulk.

(2) 49° to 54°C (120° to 130°F) then placed in containers less than 27-kg (60-lb). Time for heating and cooling is not critical. This system is well suited for the hobbyist who may wish to store small quantities of honey.

(3) 60°C (140°F) in 10 minutes, held for 30 minutes, then cooled to at least 38°C (100°F) in 10 minutes. This system is used by commercial operators who bottle honey in batches.

(4) 71°C (160°F) then cooled to 38°C (100°F) in at least 5 minutes after reaching the high temperature. Total treatment time should not exceed 10 minutes. This method suits the large scale bottling operation. With heat exchangers and temperature control devices, the operation can be highly efficient and automated.

Honey destined to be sold for home use is packed into containers 2.3 kg (5 lb) or less, and labeled to meet state and/or federal regulations. It is strained through a fine mesh screen or cloth, and heated to kill yeast cells and retard crystallization. Additional information on the effects of temperature on flavors, crystallization, and fermentation are described in Chapter 15.

BIBLIOGRAPHY

FARRAR, C.L. 1968. Productive management of honey bee colonies. Am. Bee

J. *108* (3) 95—97.

GOJMERAC, W.L. 1978. Honey: Guidelines for efficient production. Univ. of Wisconsin Ext. Publ. A 2083. Madison.

JAYCOX, E.R. 1976. Beekeeping in the Midwest. Univ. of Illinois Circ. 1125. Urbana.

MORSE, R.A. 1975. Bees and Beekeeping. Comstock Publishing Associates, Cornell University Press, Ithaca, N.Y.

OWENS, C.D., and B.F. DETROY. 1969. Selecting and operating beekeeping equipment. U.S. Dep. Agric. Bull. *2204*.

USDA. 1971. Beekeeping in the United States. U.S. Dep. Agric. Handb. 335.

9

Optional or Specialized Operations

TWO-QUEEN COLONY

The normal colony consists of one queen, a few drones, and many workers. However, it is not unusual to have a mother-daughter combination harmoniously working in the same colony. It is logical that two queens will lay more eggs than one, hence build a larger colony. The basic rationale of the two-queen colony is to develop as large a population as possible, synchronized with the major nectar flow. Initial cost of establishing a two-queen colony is the extra queen which must be purchased in spring, but the equipment investment is less per unit of honey produced. Two-queen colonies consistently produce more honey than a single queen colony and store more pollen which is of benefit the following spring. By following a systematic procedure of introducing the second queen, the majority of the colonies are automatically requeened.

The colony is divided as previously described (p. 88—90) with one colony above the other, preferably with the old queen in the lower portion. In two weeks, after the new queen is well established, the inner cover or plywood divider is replaced with a queen excluder. It allows the workers to freely intermingle, but keeps the queens separated. Each portion of the hive requires two-deep hive bodies as brood chambers, and each section of the colony is handled independently with reference to reversing. This should be done on an as-needed basis. The portions of the colony should not be switched; the upper should be maintained as the upper portion throughout the two-queen season. A two-queen colony can swarm as well as a single-queen colony if it is not properly handled.

One of the most serious disadvantages of the two-queen colony is the height of the hive. Using standard shallow equipment, at least six brood chambers and possibly six to eight honey supers are needed to adequately contain this double colony. This presents two problems: unless the colony is situated on solid, level ground or on a good foundation, it easily tips,

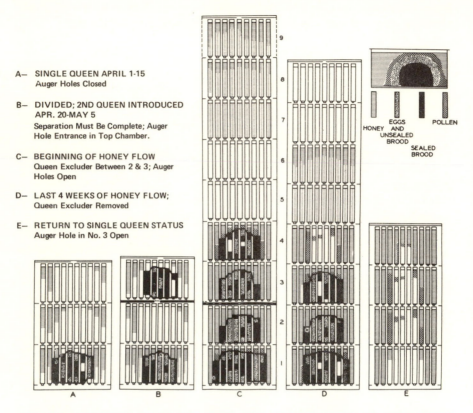

A— SINGLE QUEEN APRIL 1-15
  Auger Holes Closed

B— DIVIDED; 2ND QUEEN INTRODUCED
  APR. 20-MAY 5
  Separation Must Be Complete; Auger
  Hole Entrance in Top Chamber.

C— BEGINNING OF HONEY FLOW
  Queen Excluder Between 2 & 3; Auger
  Holes Open

D— LAST 4 WEEKS OF HONEY FLOW;
  Queen Excluder Removed

E— RETURN TO SINGLE QUEEN STATUS
  Auger Hole in No. 3 Open

HONEY   EGGS AND UNSEALED BROOD   POLLEN

SEALED BROOD

FIG. 9.1. LOCATION OF BROOD NEST AND ORGANIZATION OF TWO-QUEEN COLONY

Dates would be applicable for latitude of southern Wisconsin, northern Illinois, and other areas proportionately earlier or later.

and at this height full supers are difficult to manipulate.

Square shallow hive bodies which hold 12 standard frames have been made by some advocates of the 2-queen system. With such equipment, five hive bodies as brood chambers are adequate, two in the lower section, three above, thus lowering total colony height. While equipment manufacturers can supply such hive bodies, it is not standard equipment, and many beekeepers do not like them because they are heavier to handle when full of honey.

About three or four weeks before the normal end of the honey flow, the queen excluder is removed and the colony is reverted to single-queen status. Workers which develop from eggs laid at this time do not participate in producing honey because it takes three weeks for the worker to become an adult and two more before it forages. Observations over many years indicate that it is the younger queen which survives; thus, the now single-queen colony has been automatically requeened.

TRAPPING POLLEN

The importance of pollen to the welfare of a healthy colony is undisputed. Until a satisfactory substitute is available, beekeepers interested in operating a highly profitable operation might consider trapping pollen from some of their own colonies, extend it with either expellar process soy flour or brewer's yeast, and feed it in the spring (p. 86). It is very important that colonies selected to furnish pollen be free of foulbrood. While trapped pollen is free of disease organisms harmful to honey bees, workers removing remains of larvae which died of foulbrood could contaminate the pollen, thus spreading the disease to other colonies.

The design, construction, and operation of a pollen trap are simple. The time to operate it will vary with the locality, dependent on pollen sources and main nectar flow. Some beekeepers collect it immediately before the main nectar flow and again after; others trap it periodically throughout the season; and still others collect it continuously from a few colonies, then destroy or combine them with others for overwintering. A rule of thumb is to collect up to 0.453 kg (1 lb) per colony overwintered.

The principles common to all pollen traps are the 5-mesh hardware cloth grid (2.54 holes per cm) (5 holes per in.) or a perforated metal sheet with 4.7 mm ($^3/_{16}$ in.) holes, and a receptacle to collect the dislodged pellets as returning field workers enter the hive. Researchers and suppliers have designed a variety of traps, some to fit at the standard bottom board entrance and the auger hole. In all cases, workers should be adjusted to the entrance before the trap is put into operation.

Molds will develop on trapped pollen pellets in humid areas unless the pollen is collected daily. For the commercial operator with several yards, this means trapping in the home or nearby yard. Freshly collected pollen should be immediately frozen, dried, or blended. Freezing is the simplest if facilities are available. Drying should be done at a temperature of 43°C (110°F) or lower, then stored in air-tight containers. Pollen pellets should be crushed before blending with expellar process soy flour, as dried ones will not readily dissolve in sugar syrup. A one to one mixture of pollen and soy flour keeps the material from spoiling; additional soy flour can be added when the material is mixed for feeding.

The benefits of pollen to human nutrition are questionable. While some people continue to search for the ultimate elixer of life, there are also those who are willing to exploit any belief or idea for extravagant profits. While pollen contains proteins, carbohydrates, fats, minerals, and vitamins, analysis suggests that they are not greatly different from other

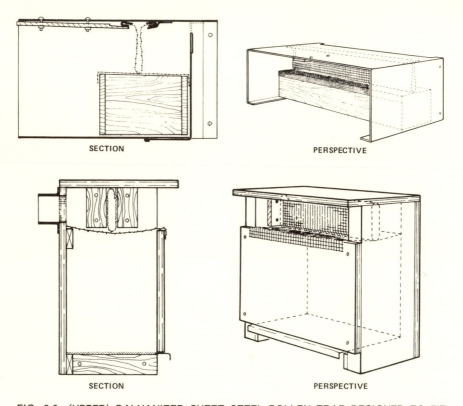

SECTION   PERSPECTIVE

SECTION   PERSPECTIVE

FIG. 9.2. *(UPPER)* GALVANIZED SHEET STEEL POLLEN TRAP DESIGNED TO FIT ACROSS THE WIDTH OF THE HIVE. *(LOWER)* WOODEN AUGER HOLE ENTRANCE POLLEN TRAP

plant proteins (see p. 62). The walls of pollen grains are tough. Some resist degradation in concentrated acids, hot alkali, and grinding. Some pollen pellets collected by bees contain microorganisms known to cause hemorrhaging, toxic mold spores, plus some dust and dirt. Placing a small quantity of pollen pellets in gelatin capsules simplifies consumption and masks the taste, but the health benefit or hazards are still to be documented.

MIGRATORY BEEKEEPING

Since ancient times, honey bees have been moved to different areas to take advantage of honey flows. Egyptians were said to have moved hives up the Nile on rafts in October and then floated them down, taking advantage of the blossoms along the way and reaching Cairo in February where the honey was sold. Today, the migratory beekeeper is highly mechanized. By placing hives on pallets and with mechanical hoists, he can easily and quickly load and unload the hives. Large flatbed trucks and truck-trailer combinations can travel long distances in a relatively short time.

In Australia, substantial numbers of colonies are moved six to eight times a season. Movements are synchronized with pollen and nectar flows which are directly associated with plant species and rainfall.

Movement in the United States is generally to the south for winter, either for colony buildup or to capitalize on specific kinds of honey such as orange blossom or sage. In spring, they are hauled north for another crop of honey. East-west movement is not as extensive and generally of shorter distance, primarily to capitalize on specific kinds of nectar.

Today many migratory beekeepers produce honey and also are in the business of providing pollination services to certain kinds of farmers. Delivering colonies at locations must be precisely synchronized with growth stage of the crop. While a large load of hives can be easily transported 643 km (400 miles) overnight, maneuvering a large truck in and around fields wet from rains or irrigation, in and over bridges and narrow culverts not suited or designed for such vehicles is difficult. While working at night simplifies problems of handling honey bees, this adds problems for drivers not familiar with the area. There are also problems and conflicts of interest with neighbors in the immediate vicinity who must use insecticides to protect their crop which at the same time kill honey bees.

Some difficulties can be avoided with advanced planning and good judgment. Transporting honey bees from one area to another sometimes requires an official inspection at the point of origin and/or a permit to enter the area or state. Migratory beekeepers must be familiar with the local regulations.

Before being loaded, hive bodies are usually tied, banded with metal tape, or secured with special staples. While it may not be necessary to close the hive entrances, most prudent beekeepers do confine honey bees even if it is only a relatively short trip. During hot weather, the top and inner cover are replaced with a screen cover. Not only would the honey bees be killed, but combs could disintegrate because of heat. Some cover the entire load with a plastic screen.

The vehicle should be in good mechanical condition and fuel tank of capacity such that a minimum number of refueling stops is required. Without such precautions, a delay or accident in route could be disastrous. Escaping honey bees would interfere with repair or servicing of the vehicle, create a serious traffic hazard, and create havoc to passing motorists or residents along the way.

Honey bees can be moved in and out of areas with very little loss to workers, provided that this is done at night. If hives are removed during the day, most of the field bees are left stranded. They can be recovered if several empty hive bodies with combs are left at the site. They will unite into one "colony" and can be recovered at a later date. But most migratory beekeepers find this to be impractical. Leaving field bees behind is not only wasteful, but they can annoy, irritate, and even sting people in the area.

BIBLIOGRAPHY

DETROY, B.F., and E.R. HARP. 1976. Trapping pollen from honey bee colonies. U.S. Dep. Agric. Prod. Res. Rep. 163.

FARRAR, C.L. 1968. Productive management of honey bee colonies. Am. Bee J. *108* (3) 95−97.

MOELLER, F.E. 1977. Two queen system of honey bee colony management. U.S. Dep. Agric. Prod. Res. Rep. 161.

10

Queen Production

Beekeepers who understand the basic biology and behavior of a colony can easily raise a few extra queens. This can be done by removing the old queen and some workers, placing them in another hive body, and allowing the colony to requeen itself. This process could also be viewed as forced or controlled swarming (p. 48).

If several queens are desired from a colony, then it is necessary to remove each large, well-formed queen cell and carefully attach it to a comb, in the natural position, in a queenless nucleus or colony. The old queen can be returned to her old hive provided all the unused queen cells are destroyed. This technique should produce four to six queens per colony.

However, this section deals primarily with the general procedure used to produce queens in a systematic fashion as a business. In 1915, G.M. Doolittle first described a simple procedure by which a large number of queens could be produced. The same basic technique, with slight modifications, is still used today.

Rearing queens is a specialized art. Those involved in the business must be committed to devoting considerable attention to details if high-quality queens are to be produced. The commercial queen rearing system, in addition to mating nuclei, involves hives designated as (1) queen breeder, (2) starter, and (3) builder.

BREEDER QUEEN

The queen mother, as breeder queens are sometimes called, should be selected from gentle colonies and preferably ones known to have queens which lay eggs in a compact or tight pattern. Disease resistance, winter hardiness, and high productivity in terms of honey and pollen storage also are characteristics everyone would like to have in their colonies. There is no reliable way to insure that these traits are present. Some of these characteristics are extremely difficult to measure. Reputable queen producers should always be on the lookout for colonies which are outstanding performers or have desirable traits, in their own yards, or be willing to purchase stock of known quality from others, including genetic lines developed by government laboratories available from the stock centers.

The breeder queen is confined in a standard hive which has been modified with queen excluder material so that she is forced to lay eggs only on one comb during a specific time period or day. The comb should be dark so that eggs are easily visible. Each day a different comb is given to the queen and the previous one placed in another part of the hive to incubate. On the third day, eggs will begin to hatch, and when larvae are about 12 hours old they are ready for transfer. Transferring larvae from one cell to another is referred to as grafting, which was first done in 1791 by Francis Huber.

Beekeeping suppliers sell queen cup cells, but many queen producers make their own during the off-season. These cells are simply a wax base, shaped like the beginnings of a swarm cell, on which workers build the queen cell. Wooden pegs 9.5 mm (⅜ in.) rounded at one end can be used as a form on which to build them. First dipping the tip in a mild soap solution, then five to six times into melted beeswax, and allowing it to solidify produces excellent cup cells. The soap solution allows the cup to be easily detached from the peg. Washing in cool water removes traces of soap from inside the cell.

Before grafting, 10 or 12 cup cells are attached with beeswax to a queen cell bar, which is a piece of wood cut to fit in the lower part of a standard frame. The grafted cup cells hang vertically at the middle or lower edge of a frame somewhat like swarm cells. Just before grafting, a little royal jelly diluted with warm water is placed in each cup. This liquid keeps the grafted larvae from drying and helps to detach it from the grafting needle, which is a thin rod with a hook on one end. Grafting must be done in a warm, 23.9°C (75°F), or warmer room. Close observations and controlled experiments over many years suggest that grafted larvae should be about 12 hours old, but not older than 18 hours, if quality queens are to be produced.

Immediately after grafting, the cell bar with queen cup cells is placed in the starter hive. The starter hive should have an adequate supply of pollen and nectar. It also should have an abundant supply of young workers and be kept queenless. A population of young workers can be assured if frames of mature brood are periodically transferred into this hive. Nurse bees will feed these newly grafted larvae and begin to raise them as queens. After 24 hours, the larvae are examined. Those not accepted are replaced with others and then transferred to the cell builder hive. Here young workers continue feeding the developing queens until the cells are sealed.

Some queen producers utilize a system of double grafting. After the initial grafts are in a starter hive for 24 hours, the larvae are discarded and new ones are placed in the royal jelly. This second batch has a more abundant supply of royal jelly, and by controlled experiments it can be demonstrated that superior queens are produced by this method. Since additional labor is invested, the queens are more costly.

BUILDER HIVES

These are somewhat larger than starter hives. Unless a good nectar flow is underway, the colony should be fed sugar syrup in a division board feeder and also have pollen or pollen substitutes available. It should be inspected about every ten days to assure an adequate supply of food. The queen should be confined with a queen excluder to the lower chamber, and unsealed brood moved upward to attract young workers to the top. Sealed brood is transferred downward. The builder hive should basically be kept in a preswarm condition; that is, the upper portion kept crowded with young workers and unsealed brood. The queen cell bar with developing queens should be placed towards the center of the hive so that they are kept warm and well fed. Overstocking the starter or builder hive with too many queen cup cells will produce inferior queens. Allowing workers in either hive to become too old also reduces the quality of the queens (p. 35).

Queen cells are normally sealed in five days after hatching, or eight days after the egg is deposited. Once sealed, they can be removed from the builder hive either to an incubator set at 32.2°C (90°F) or to mating nuclei. Recently sealed cells are quite delicate and must be kept warm and handled with care; for this reason, some allow them to remain in the builder hive until a day or two prior to emergence. The standard procedure is to move queen cells to nuclei ten days after grafting.

MATING NUCLEI

These are specially constructed hives with a small population of workers supplied with a small feeder containing sugar syrup or a comb of honey and pollen. While they can be any shape or size, some use a standard hive body, divided into three separate compartments, each with its own entrance facing in a different direction. The queen cell is introduced into the nucleus by carefully attaching it to one of the frames in a natural position, so that she can emerge, mate, and begin to lay. One mating yard may contain as many as 1,500 to 2,000 nuclei, so some queen producers provide the yard with one or several colonies which contain a large number of drones. While it might be a good practice for the producer to raise some drones for his operation, there is no way to assure the buyer that his queens were mated with a specific type of drone, unless the yard was completely isolated not only from other beekeepers, but also from wild honey bees established in a hollow tree or other similar cavity. In about 14 days after the queen cell is placed in a nucleus, she should be laying and is ready to be caged and shipped. At that time another queen cell can be introduced into the nucleus. In many operations, a queen producer can utilize technicians; however, the individual choosing queens for shipping should be able to visually evaluate or judge each one. The ideal queen should be free of any deformity or defect, large in size, loosely jointed between the thorax and abdomen, and carry her abdomen off the surface. She should remain docile on the comb, rather than attempt to fly off, and the brood pattern should be compact. Queens not measuring up to these standards should not be sold.

Unfortunately, queen producers are sometimes put under pressure by circumstances beyond their control. Unseasonably cold weather early in the spring or rainy periods might interfere with or prevent natural matings, thus upsetting the schedule and preventing delivery on time.

Tested queens are those which are known to be fertilized as judged by brood pattern. While it is legal to sell untested ones, the buyer should be aware of what is being purchased. Many queens are superceded prematurely because of nosema disease. Prudent queen producers should have an active control program using the approved drug fumigillan (see p. 138).

The method of storing queens prior to shipping varies with the producer, size of operation, and facilities. They can be left in mating nuclei, if space is available, or stored in queen banks. A queen bank colony may contain several hundred queens, each alone in her individual cage, being fed through the wire screen by workers from the colony. This colony should not have a laying queen as she will attempt to fight or sting the others, even through the screen. Queens can be stored in banks for a month or longer after mating.

When an order is received, the queen is transferred to a mailing cage along with several attendants (workers) and queen candy as food. The practice of shipping queens by mail was first done in 1863, when one was sent from New York to Ohio. The standard mailing cage used today was perfected in 1883. It is made from a block of wood with three connecting round holes. One serves as a container for food and the other two as compartments for the queen and attendants. Queen candy is simply a firm mixture of invert sugar and starch-free powdered sugar. Queens can be safely kept in these cages up to two weeks, provided they are protected from extremes in temperature. A drop of water is occasionally added. Some buyers of queens prefer to ship or transport them in a queen cage carrier. Two standard frames are modified to hold 36 cages, and a third frame contains honey. These three frames are placed in a standard nuc box, or specially designed hive body, with about 0.98 kg (1.5 lb) workers. If the weather is hot, the cage carrier should have a screened cover.

One large cell builder hive is capable of producing 200 to 400 queens per month. Such an operation can supply between 100 and 200 mating nuclei, and the average queen producer can expect to obtain 50 mated queens for every 100 queen cells introduced. This reemphasizes the initial statement that producing queens is a highly technical operation well suited for the person who is interested in paying close attention to details.

The success of a queen-rearing business not only depends on understanding the basic biology and behavior of the honey bee colony, but relies heavily on developing an efficient system of managing and fully utilizing skilled labor and capital. Schedules for grafting, for example, must not only be synchronized with conditions of the starter and builder colonies, but with availability of technicians for weekend or holiday work.

CONTROLLED BREEDING

It is with instrument insemination that man is able to control the breeding of honey bees. This involves obtaining the semen from drones and placing it inside the queen with instruments. Since queens always mate away from the hive, in flight, natural matings cannot be controlled unless all drones in the area are also under control. Controlled natural matings have been performed on isolated small islands, and in isolated mountain meadows; however, such locations are very limited. Matings will not occur in enclosed areas.

First attempts to develop instrument insemination began nearly 200 years ago, but were not successful because the structure and function of the reproductive system was not completely understood. In about 1920, enough was known about the queen's anatomy to start the development of a workable technique. By the late 1930's, it was recognized that not enough semen was collected, and that a small valve flap was preventing it from being placed deep into the spermatheca, a sperm storage structure in the queen. In the late 1940's, it was discovered that carbon dioxide, used as an anesthetic, hastened the onset of egg laying in the queen. As these basic discoveries were being made, finer and more delicate instruments and queen holding devices were also developed.

Natural matings of honey bees have been difficult to study, so information had to be obtained by observing queens immediately after they

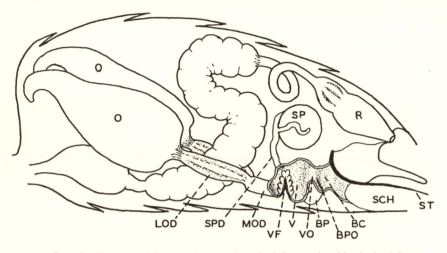

Reproductive organs of the queen in approximately their natural position in the abdomen, with left side of vagina and bursa copulatrix cut away: BC, bursa copulatrix; BP, right bursal pouch; BPO, opening to bursal pouch; LOD, lateral oviduct; MOD, median oviduct; O, ovary; R, rectum; SCH, sting chamber; SP, spermatheca; SPD, spermathecal duct; ST, sting; V, vagina; VF, valvefold; VO, vaginal orifice.

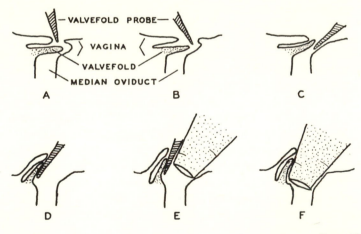

FIG. 10.1. REPRODUCTIVE SYSTEM IN QUEEN HONEY BEE AND MANNER OF PUSHING ASIDE THE VALVE FLAP SO SEMEN CAN ENTER SPERMATHECAL DUCT

returned to the hive from mating flights. Normally both oviducts are distended, being filled with semen, but after six to seven hours, most of the sperm is in the spermatheca. The exact manner in which this happens is not fully understood. A naturally mated queen receives about 11.6 microliters (maximum 28) of semen which suggests that she mated with 8 or 9 drones. The estimated maximum number of drones is 17.

The exact procedures used in instrument insemination are described by Mackensen and Tucker (1970). While it is possible to learn the technique by studying detailed descriptions, the most efficient way to become proficient is to work under the guidance of an experienced operator. The technician should have a functional understanding of the queen's anatomy, and be aware of the following principles. (1) Some queens are easier to inseminate than others; therefore a novice should consider obtaining queens from several breeders. (2) Large queens are easier to inseminate than small ones. (3) Queens that have been free to run in a queen nucleus and are about six or seven days old are easier to handle than those held in small cages. (4) Insemination should be done in a warm, humid atmosphere; however, once experienced, the operator may be able to work fast enough to prevent tissues from drying.

For research purposes and in controlled breeding, it may be necessary or highly desirable to inseminate a queen with semen from a single drone. Such queens must be confined to their brood nest with a queen excluder, otherwise they might fly out and also mate naturally. Such queens may lay only for a short time (months) before being "naturally" superceded. Instrumentally inseminated queens destined to head a large or full size colony should receive at least 5 million sperm cells (8 microliters of semen). An experienced technician should be able to have about 90% of the queens laying as good as those naturally mated, somewhat less with single drone matings.

With the perfection of instrument insemination, the possibilities of developing hybrids became a reality. This involves a period of inbreeding, then selecting inbred lines with desirable traits for crossing. Rapid inbreeding can be obtained by allowing the queen to first produce some drones, then using their semen to inseminate her. Genetically, this is self-fertilization, because the drones represent only the queen's gametes, as they developed from her unfertilized eggs. While this method gives a rapid rate of inbreeding, the offspring often exhibit low breed viability, so other methods of line inbreeding are generally used. Slower inbreeding produces a more vigorous stock on which to make evaluations, measurements, and observations than the crosses. The offspring of the crosses would contain the desired characteristics and hybrid vigor.

Hybrids and inbreds have been evaluated over the years at the U.S. Department of Agriculture laboratories. Queen productivity is measured by square inches of brood at a specific time. Resistance to American foulbrood is measured by inserting a diseased comb in a healthy colony.

While some hybrids were found to be resistant to foulbrood, they were so defensive that the lines were discontinued.

Many characteristics not found in normal colonies are expressed in inbred lines. In addition to the highly defensive characteristics mentioned, other lines are extremely gentle or docile, almost to the point where they refuse to sting, even when disturbed or provoked. Workers of some lines take flight as soon as the comb is removed from the hive. Others will run around on it, and always appear extremely nervous, but not leave it. Some build extensive quantities of bur and brace comb, and one line refused to build comb on foundations, but destroyed it, then built its own foundation and comb. One line refused to cap honey, and some lines will build wax caps in direct contact with honey, so the capped comb looks wet. Others will leave a little air space between the honey and wax so the cap is white. Some lines even have been known to prefer a specific pollen source, such as alfalfa and/or cranberries, which would be a desirable trait in colonies used in pollination services.

Through the years, man has selected and crossed many desirable plants and animals to suit his interests and needs. The honey bee breeder can utilize the same basic rules of genetics, mainly inbreeding and selection, then crosses to obtain a product designed to suit his interests and/or needs. But inbreeding, selecting, and maintaining inbred lines of honey bees are expensive. The queens are basically inferior and easily superceded, and overwintering in northern areas is poor. Inbred lines have been developed and are maintained at the U.S. Department of Agriculture laboratories. Commercial queen breeders are able to purchase stock and use it for their own operations. While the honey bee breeder started late, progress has been rapid and the potential for future developments is very promising. The breeder will probably be able to design a honey bee to suit the interests and needs of the beekeepers.

BIBLIOGRAPHY

GONCALVES, L.L., and A.C. STORT. 1978. Honey bee improvement through behavioral genetics. Ann. Rev. Entomol. *23*, p.197-213.

LAIDLAW, H.H., JR., and J.E. ECKERT. 1962. Queen Rearing. Univ. of California Press, Berkeley.

MACKENSEN, O., and K. W. TUCKER. 1970. Instrumental insemination of queen bees. U.S. Dep. Agric. Handb. 390.

MOELLER, F.E. 1976. Development of hybrid honey bees. U.S. Dep. Agric. Prod. Res. Rep. 168.

NYE, W.P., and D. MACKENSEN. 1970. Selective breeding of honey bees for alfalfa pollen collection: with tests in high and low alfalfa pollen collection regions. J. Apic. Res. *9* (2) 61-64.

ROTHENBUHLER, W.C.   1958.   Genetics and breeding of the honey bee. Ann. Rev. Entomol. *3*, p.161-180.

TABERS, S., and M.S. BLUM.   1960.   Preservation of honey bee semen. Science *131* (3415) 1734-1735.

11

Hive Products Other Than Honey

BEESWAX

Three different kinds of waxes are found in nature: animal, plant, and mineral or petroleum. Beeswax, an animal wax, is a very stable mixture of chemicals with a distinguished history. It has been found in Egyptian tombs and washed ashore from ancient shipwrecks. Man's first and only plastic for many years, it commanded a high price, and in some areas it served as a medium of exchange. Architects used beeswax to model proposed structures, sailors to strengthen and waterproof sails and lines, and soldiers to waterproof tenting and food storage containers. More recently it was used to waterproof and insulate electrical instruments and coat munitions, make dental impressions, stiffen and strengthen sewing threads, as well as a long list of highly specialized uses such as mustache, ski, and snowshoe wax, and polishes for wood and metal.

Major users of beeswax today include the cosmetic, candlemaking, and beekeeping industries. Many of the formulas for cold creams, ointments, lotions, pomades, lipsticks, rouges, salves, and pill coatings contain beeswax. Some adhesives, crayons, chewing gums, and inks also contain beeswax.

Church candles utilize a substantial quantity of beeswax not only for its symbolic meaning, but because it burns with a slow, smokeless flame and emits a pleasing odor. At one time, church regulations specified that candles had to be made from pure beeswax. However, due to shortages, blends are currently permitted.

Substantial quantity of beeswax is used by the beekeeping industry for new and replacement foundation. Some beekeepers lament the fact that their industry lost some important uses of beeswax to petroleum paraffin, plant waxes, and plastics. Realistically, if all competing materials were eliminated, the beekeeping industry could not supply the quantity needed to meet the demands of society today.

PHYSICAL PROPERTIES

The melting point of pure beeswax ranges between 61° and 69°C (142° and 156°F), refractive index 1.44, dielectric constant 2.9, and density 0.96 at 20°C (68°F). It is insoluble in water, but slightly soluble in cold alcohol. Benzene chloroform, carbon disulfide, ether, and some volatile oils will completely dissolve beeswax. It has a faint but characteristic odor and taste, and burns with a clean yellow flame, emitting its own unique aroma. The properties of freshly secreted beeswax are fairly constant, but beeswax is contaminated to varying degrees by pollen, propolis, and honey, which increases its density and color. Color in beeswax is derived from pigments contained in pollen and propolis and/or iron oxide from contact with metallic iron.

CHEMICAL CHARACTERISTICS

Beeswax is a highly complex mixture of organic chemicals, comprised of 12 to 14% straight chain, odd-numbered hydrocarbons C_{21} to C_{33}. The total ester component is 64% of which mono-, di-, and triesters comprise 35, 14, and 3%, respectively, and hydroxy mono- and polyesters are 4 and 8%. It also contains 12% free acids, and 3% acid esters plus 6 to 7% unidentified substances. The monohydric alcohols are C_{24} to C_{36}, diols C_{24} to C_{32}, and acid C_{12} to C_{34}, and hydroxyacids C_{12} to C_{32}. Some textbooks state that beeswax is an ester of palmitic and cerotic acid. This is an over-simplification of a highly complex material.

Paraffin waxes, derived from petroleum oil, resemble beeswax in some characteristics. The melting point and other physical properties are, in part, determined by molecular structure and configuration. Paraffin molecules are straight or branched chains, saturated hydrocarbons, free of acids, aromatic, and unsaturated compounds, and chemically, a much simpler mixture.

PROCESSING BEESWAX

Cappings of sealed honey yield between 0.453 and 0.906 kg (1 and 2 lb) of beeswax per 43.5 kg (100 lb) of extracted honey. Because of solubility, low melting point, and specific gravity, beeswax can be easily separated from honey and other foreign matter. After draining or centrifuging the bulk of honey from cappings, heating the remains between 66° and 71°C (150° and 160°F) melts the beeswax, which floats on the remaining honey, and when cooled, it can be lifted off. Beekeeping equipment suppliers have a variety of devices to handle cappings, all basically using the same principle of heat and specific gravity. Because honey as well as beeswax can be damaged by excessive heat, accurate temperature controls are required on the equipment.

Liquid beeswax can be siphoned, drained, or poured into molds. Foreign matter consisting of dirt, dust, pollen, propolis, and resins will settle to the bottom of the tank or mold. If high quality beeswax is desired, this residue, called slum gum, should be kept separate. Some wax processors will purchase it, the price determined by the amount of wax recovered.

Rendering old combs is more involved. It is possible to recover between 0.906 and 1.3 kg (2 and 3 lb) of wax from one standard hive body of old, distorted, or damaged combs. Brood combs will contain cast skins and pupal cases of immature honey bees in addition to other dirt, pollen, and propolis. Melting combs in hot water, then straining the contents through a fine mesh screen or cloth separates the debris from the beeswax. After cooling, the wax can be lifted from the surface of the water. The debris can be "washed" in hot water several times to recover additional beeswax.

Larger operators immerse combs in sacks in a container of hot water, allowing the beeswax to float to the surface or place the material to be rendered in a hot water or steam press. Solar extraction may be ecologically sound, but it recovers only about 50% of the available wax from a comb.

Wax processors are interested in obtaining as high a quality product as possible from beekeepers. While facilities are available to refine beeswax of any quality, they are interested in keeping beekeepers from damaging or lowering the quality of the product through ignorance. They suggest beeswax from American foulbrood-infected hives not be sold. Some states require burning of diseased equipment and others prohibit selling of such beeswax. While such beeswax might safely be made into candles, should foundation be made of this material, the disease would be further spread. Processing beeswax does not kill spores of this disease.

They also recommend that scrappage from equipment which contains large amounts of propolis and resins be kept separate from capping wax. Iron and some metals such as zinc, brass, and copper tend to darken beeswax. Buyers pay a premium price for light-colored wax, which is used in the cosmetic and church candle industry. Filtered wax would be used for section comb honey and possibly dental impressions. The water-washed product usually is made into regular foundation purchased by beekeepers.

PROPOLIS

Propolis is the sticky, resinous material gathered by workers from buds and bark of trees, and possibly from other vegetation. Foraging workers also have been known to bring in synthetic sticky material such as caulking compound and wet paint. Within the hive it serves a useful purpose. However, beekeepers, especially in the United States, consider it a nuisance. It sticks to hands, clothing, shoes, and tools in warm weather; and when it is cold, propolis is hard and brittle. Removing it from hive bodies and frames requires extra labor.

Propolis is a highly complex mixture of waxes, resins, balsams, oils, and a small amount of pollen. Its composition is highly variable, probably related to the species of plants from which it is collected.

In the hive, propolis is used to fill cracks and crevices, varnish over rough surfaces, and reduce or close openings to the outside.

It is considered a contaminant in beeswax. Years ago, famous violin makers in Italy, including Stradivarius, used this substance as an ingredient in his varnish.

Europeans have taken a greater interest in propolis than people in other countries, although some in the United States advocate further research, with the hopes of finding a market for what is now generally thought to be a useless or nuisance product. Several Europeans have found propolis to have bactericidal, bacteriostatic, and antibiotic properties. However, critics maintain that much of the research or tests is of questionable value. There are reports that extracts of propolis will heal wounds, cure foot and mouth disease in cattle, kill influenza virus, and aid in the treatment of skin diseases. A dentist in Russia reported a two to four percent extract is three to five times more effective as an anaesthetic than cocaine. Based on what is known today, some of these claims may be true, because propolis contains a mixture of many chemicals. But verifying or duplicating test results, using such a highly variable and complex product as propolis, is challenging. While no market for it exists in the United States today, beekeepers would be ready to supply the material if one were to develop.

ROYAL JELLY

The characteristics, composition, and some questionable uses of royal jelly were described on p. 33. Queen producers require it in their operation and must collect it from developing queen cells or purchase some from other beekeepers. Royal jelly can be removed from developing queen cells with a small spoon or aspirator.

On a large scale, royal jelly can be produced in builder hives, previously described (p. 105). Queen cup cells are placed in a builder colony. At the end of the third day, each queen cup cell will contain about 200 mg (0.07 oz) of royal jelly and a developing queen larva. The larva is removed with a small needle or forceps and is discarded. Then the royal jelly is removed with a spoon or aspirator. It is strained through a fine (100-mesh) nylon cloth and stored in a refrigerator at 0.6° to 1.7°C (33° to 35°F) if it is to be used within 1 or 2 weeks. For long term storage it should be frozen. The 1978 price, as advertised in beekeeping trade journals, was about $120.00 per 0.453 kg (1 lb).

PACKAGED BEES

It was in 1879 that A.I. Root, in Ohio, conceived of the idea and first tried shipping honey bees in a screened cage without the usual combs and supply of honey. Shipping weights for the standard 1.35-kg (3-lb) package were reduced from 18.1 or 22.6 kg (40 or 50 lb) to 2.3 or 2.7 kg (5 or 6 lb). This development provided an economical and simple way for beginners to get started with honey bees, and essentially advanced the active honey producing season for residents in northern parts of the country. The first large scale shipment of packages was made in 1912 from Alabama.

With modern means of transportation, packages can be shipped long distances in cages (packages). The honey bees are provided with a supply of sugar syrup and protected from the extremes of heat and cold. Package weights have been standardized to 0.9, 1.3, 1.8, and 2.2 kg (2, 3, 4, and 5 lb). The larger ones are sometimes available on special order for use in pollination. One pound (0.453 kg) contains between 3,300 and 4,400 workers, depending on the degree of engorging which preceded weighing. Some states require a health certificate from the state of origin.

Producing package bees provides an additional source of income for some migratory beekeepers, and is the major occupation for others. Management of colonies intended for package bee production is not substantially different from colonies destined to produce honey. Timing is critical. Most packages are shipped during late March, April, and early May. The package producer's season begins in late August, and colony build-up has to begin in January and February. Periodically removing workers reduces honey storage potential, but the colony utilizes substantial quantities of pollen and nectar in the production of bees.

Packages are sold with or without queens, but producers who do not raise their own usually contract for a supply from queen producers.

To fill packages from a hive, the queen is removed or confined to the lower hive body. If she is removed temporarily, workers can be shaken from individual frames through a funnel into the cage, through the opening designed to hold the feeder can. If the queen is confined to the lower chambers, rhythmically tapping the hive with the hand or rubber mallet (drumming) entices workers to move upward through the queen excluder. From here, they can be shaken off the frames into the funnel. Large operators will have labor-saving devices such as stands, carts, etc.; however, there is no simple way to automate this operation.

With a normal hive, it is possible to remove about 1.8 kg (4 lb) of bees per 10-day intervals without weakening the colony. Experimental colonies have produced 14.5 kg (32 lb) of workers over a 60-day period. However, most commercial package producers remove about 4.53 kg (10 lb) per colony each season.

After weighing, a queen (if ordered) is suspended in the package in her mailing cage, and the feeder can, with sugar syrup, is secured in the special opening. Cages can be crated together with wood laths for spacing and easier handling, usually in multiples of three or in quantities and dimensions to fit the vehicle. Packages should be stacked in the truck so that there will be sufficient ventilation, at least 14.7 cm (6 in.) between packages and the sides and top of the stack. Closed vehicles should have an airflow from the front to rear with provisions to close the vents if cold weather is encountered during the trip.

Packages to hobbyists generally are shipped by parcel post, but many part-time and commercial operators prefer to pick up their orders. Beekeeping equipment dealers often combine orders from a number of hobbyists and then contract with a trucker for delivery to a location on a specific date.

The business of package bees evolved through the years so that delivery can be expected within one or two days of scheduling. The producer's season is short, so most producers sell on advanced booking basis, requesting a deposit with the order, with balance due at the time of or before shipping. Reputable suppliers usually deliver confirmed orders on time, with late orders handled in sequence.

BIBLIOGRAPHY

BISSON, C.S., G.H. VANSELL, and W.B. DYE. 1940. Investigations on the physical and chemical properties of beeswax. U.S. Dep. Agric. Tech. Bull. *716*.

BLUM, M.S., A.F. NOVAK, and S. TABER, III. 1959. 10-hydroxy Δdeconoic acid, an antibiotic found in royal jelly. Science *130* (3373) 452-453.

JACKSON, L.L., and G.J. BLOMQUIST. 1976. Insect waxes. *In* Chemistry and Biochemistry of Natural Waxes. P.E. Kolattukudy (Editor). Elsevier, New York.

WITHERELL, P. 1975. Other products from the hive. *In* The Hive and the Honey Bee. Edited and published by Dadant and Sons, Hamilton, Ill.

YORK, H.E., JR. 1975. Production of queens and package bees. *In* The Hive and the Honey Bee. Edited and published by Dadant and Sons, Hamilton, Ill.

12

Pollination

Pollination is essential to the survival of the species. It is accomplished inconspicuously, so that it is often ignored, overlooked, or left to chance. In some cases, insufficient pollination can mean the difference between a profit or loss to the farmer. Pollination is a complex process influenced by overlapping factors such as temperature, moisture, nutrition of the crop, and the availability of pollinators. Although some of these factors cannot be controlled, others can be influenced by the farmer. This chapter is not intended to discuss the technical details of pollination, but to explain some of the interrelationships between the crops requiring pollination and the honey bee colony.

Pollination is the mechanical transfer of pollen from the anther to the stigma of the flower. This can be accomplished by several methods; the most common methods are by insects and wind. Fertilization sometimes is confused with pollination. This occurs after the pollen (male) grain germinates and its nucleus unites with the ovule (female), forming the seed. Cross pollination occurs when pollen is transferred from one variety to another, and self-pollination refers to the transfer of pollen from the anther to the stigma on the same flower, other flowers on the same plant, or another plant of the same variety.

The importance of cross pollination was recognized long before its biological significance was understood. There is some evidence from 1500 B.C. which is interpreted as someone holding staminate (male) date palm flowers over the pistillate (female) one. More recently (about 682 A.D.) an Arabic writer was quoted as saying that the date palm *(Phoenix dactylifera)* had to be artificially fertilized. The date palm is dioecious (male and female plants) and pollen must be transferred from the male tree to the female. In nature, this is done by wind. However, to obtain higher yields, staminate flowers are excised and pollen dusted over the pistillate ones. Yet the idea of cross pollination was not associated with other plants until the 1680's.

It is also supposed, from time immemorial, that Chinese and Japanese gardeners developed asters, camellias, and many other flowers which are the results of cross pollination. It is also assumed that they dusted pollen from one blossoming plant to another, but there are no documented records to support this conclusion.

In 1682, N. Grew, a botanist, stated that pollen must reach the stigma before seeds develop, and it was in the 1760's before it was realized that bees and other insects could transfer pollen. In 1799, Thomas Andrew Knight showed the value of cross pollination and associated it with hybrid vigor. He postulated that nature adapted the pollen to adhere to insect bodies, and finally it was Charles Darwin, in 1899, who proved and popularized the importance of pollination in the maintenance of vigor and perpetuation of the species.

In the United States, M.B. Waite, in 1895, discovered the phenomenon of self-sterility in pears *(Pyrus)* and demonstrated the need for insects transferring pollen among varieties. About this time, beekeeping trade journals began to publicize the values and virtues of the honey bee as a pollinating creature and a honey producer. It was in 1909 when the more progressive and innovative growers began to rent colonies of bees for pollination.

The honey bee is responsible for providing some parts of the world with a more varied and healthful diet. While rice, wheat, beans, and corn, which are self- or wind-pollinated, provide the staple food, fruits, vegetables, and some livestock products provide the variety and are, to a large degree, dependent on honey bees for pollination, indirectly or directly.

It is for history to decide whether American agriculture opened a new era for the honey bee. Without doubt, the honey bee today is more valuable to mankind as a pollinator than a honey producer. While some other insects and a few animals are instrumental in pollinating some plants, based on what is known today, no other pollinating insect can be as easily managed and manipulated as the honey bee. It is for this reason it will continue to be recognized as an important insect.

Agricultural economists and statisticians are able to measure acres and assign values to the crops which benefit or require insect pollination. While they are impressive, most reasonable people understand and recognize that these values are not precise; but people accept the fact that honey bees are important. A simplistic, yet fairly accurate estimate of the value of the honey bee's role in food production is that approximately one-third of our food supply is either directly or indirectly dependent on insect-pollinated plants. Livestock products such as milk, eggs, butter, meat, and cheese are foods generally indirectly dependent on insect pollination, as animal forage crops such as alfalfa and clovers require pollination.

There are indirect benefits from pollination as performed by the honey bee. Legumes are capable of fixing nitrogen, thereby enriching the soil. Without legumes, soils in many areas would be quickly depleted and become unproductive. One factor contributing to the abundant food supply in the United States is the efficient production system. Inadequately pollinated plants will have an uneven fruit or seed set, in some cases misshaped or deformed produce, and crops which mature over a long period of time. On the other hand, adequate pollination usually assures a uniform quality and even maturity which is well suited for a large-scale, efficient operation.

American agriculture has undergone a revolution within the last half century. The average farmer, utilizing large and highly efficient machines and employing the latest technology, is able to produce enough food for about 50 people. To achieve this efficiency, the farmer had to resort to mono-culture, use insecticides, and remove hedge and fence rows, thus destroying many native pollinators. Farmers growing crops which require cross pollination find it profitable to include pollinating honey bees as an "input" in their operation.

MANAGING COLONIES FOR POLLINATION

Handling a colony destined for pollination is not greatly different from handling one for honey production. Large or strong colonies are preferred over small ones. Colonies with a large percentage of eggs or young larvae in the brood chamber will forage more intensely for pollen, and so will one which has empty, dark comb available for pollen storage. Manipulations which encourage brood rearing are of benefit to the pollination colony. It is the old workers which forage; therefore a colony composed of young workers will be less efficient than one composed of old ones. While these factors are difficult to regulate, the beekeeper does have control over colony size. However, there are no official standards other than the integrity or reputation of the beekeeper.

A single-story colony rented or sold for pollination purposes should have a full hive body of honey bees and about six frames of brood. As each frame is lifted out, it should be covered with workers. A two-story colony should have six to ten frames of brood. If the colony is divided in the middle, both surfaces should be covered with a blanket of workers. In several days, each type of colony would be ready to receive an additional hive body or honey super. A three-story hive of shallow equipment is about equivalent to a two-story deep hive and should contain eight to twelve frames of brood.

POLLINATION PROBLEMS

Honey bees have a hierarchy of preference for specific flowers. They are opportunists and have no way of knowing man's interests or needs and do not distinguish between weeds and cultivated crops. It is believed that sugar concentration and balance among glucose, fructose, and sucrose influence foragers to prefer one species over the other. For example, nectar of pear is low in sugar (5 to 10%) while apple, yellow rocket, and dandelion, which bloom about the same time, produce nectar which contains about 40% sugars. Foraging workers have been known to abandon pears for these other plants. Sugar content of sweet and red clover is not dramatically different, but foragers prefer sweet clover, probably because of the more favorable balance of sugar.

In some situations, farmers can reduce or eliminate some competing plants. For example, clovers and blackberries bloom about the same time as cranberries. Eliminating them from ditch-banks and roadways might improve pollination of cranberries. A more effective way to cope with the competing plant problem is by colony movement. If they are moved more than two miles from the old location, workers need to reorient themselves. At the new site, they begin foraging in a matter of hours. If movement into the area is delayed until 15 to 20% of the blossoms are open and colonies are interspersed among the crop, pollination will be more complete than if colonies are moved in advance of blossom time. This procedure will give foragers less time to find competing plants. Temperature at blossom time is also critical, especially for early blooming crops such as apples, pears, and almonds. There is very little the beekeeper or farmer can do to correct the problem (see p. 44). Normally, a worker confines foraging for nectar and/or pollen to one species of plant at a time. But this flower fidelity works against cross pollination, especially with some hybrids. For example: One variety may produce abundant pollen with little nectar, while another may produce little pollen but abundant nectar. The pollen foragers tend to confine their activity to one variety while those gathering nectar stay with the other with very little crossover which the farmer requires.

Workers tend to confine their foraging to a relatively small area. With plants such as the clovers and alfalfa, and vine crops such as cucumbers and melons which are relatively small, this presents no serious problem. But with some large trees, the situation is a little different. To adequately cross pollinate the crop, foragers must move from tree to tree rather than forage exclusively on one tree.

The mechanics of handling and using honey bees for pollination will vary with the crop. Prudent beekeepers as well as growers usually establish a contractual relationship. Some agreed-upon items include (1) rental price per colony, (2) delivery time, (3) number and strength of colonies, (4) placement and management of colonies during pollination, (5) protection of honey bees from farming operations, such as irrigation and insecticide sprays, (6) colony removal after pollination, and (7) liability from sting.

While much is known about colony management and its relationship to pollination, further studies are needed to accurately define pollination requirements to potential crop production. In many situations it is standard practice to recommend between one and six colonies per unit area (hectare-acre), but the experimental basis for such figures, in many cases, has never been established. Crop production practices, varieties, and even consumer preferences change so there is a need to continually reevaluate pollination requirements.

CHALLENGES

To illustrate several unique problems and challenges facing agriculture, an overview of the pollination needs for three crops, alfalfa, almonds, and soybeans, will be given. Additional information on pollination is contained in the U.S. Department of Agriculture Handbook No. 496, compiled by McGregor (1976).

Alfalfa *(Medicago sativa)* is an extremely important forage crop grown world-wide for its high quality protein and soil building and holding capabilities. This crop is also important to beekeepers because it produces an abundant quantity of high quality nectar. But when alfalfa is grown exclusively as a forage crop under good management practices, little nectar is harvested because it is cut before significant bloom occurs (p. 150). While these farmers have no reason to be interested in pollination, honey bees affect their welfare because the farmers must purchase costly seed. One way to lower the price is to increase efficiency, by obtaining a higher yield per acre. Practically all alfalfa seed for the United States is grown in the western part of the country, because of the longer growing season, soil type, and low humidity. One limiting factor in efficient seed production is proper pollination and it is for this reason alfalfa pollination has been studied in considerable detail in the United States and also in foreign countries.

The alfalfa flower is unique in that it must be tripped before it can be pollinated. This was known as far back as 1867. The corolla (flower petals) is modified into two wing or standard petals, and two that are fused into a single structure, the keel. The keel encloses ten anthers, stigma, style, and ovary. These flower parts are held under tension and are non-functional until released from the keel. This can be accomplished by rough treatment of the plant, such as a strong wind, focusing the sun's rays through a magnifying glass into the flower, and by pollinating insects. Insects smaller than 64 mm (¼ in.) generally do not trip the flower, but honey bees, leaf cutters, and alkali bees will trip it in search of nectar. The latter two are very efficient trippers and pollinators. As a foraging bee enters the flower and presses her head against the standard petal to obtain nectar, the lower part of the flower (keel) snaps open, and the anthers and style strike and dust her with pollen. As she moves to another flower in search of nectar, the process is repeated, transferring pollen from her body to the stigma, and thus completing pollination. Honey bees apparently do not like to be struck by this mechanism and eventually learn to obtain nectar without tripping the flower. But until she learns how to avoid being struck, she has pollinated a number of flowers. So it is generally the young foragers which are efficient pollinators of alfalfa, and the old ones continue to gather nectar. Fewer than one percent of the self-tripped, and none of the non-tripped flowers, produce seed. Researchers have tried to trip flowers mechanically by such devices as dragging a rope, chain, brushes, or rollers over plants, and even hiring a helicopter to help the process. Self- and easily-tripped strains (cultivars) have been developed, but such lines degenerate rapidly.

Over the years, there have been differences of opinion as to the value honey bees play in pollinating alfalfa. Up to 1946, most believed they played a minor or insignificant role, but more precise experiments now indicate that honey bees serve as an essential pollinator in many areas. In 1951, convincing evidence was obtained to prove beyond doubt that the honey bee was a valuable pollinator of alfalfa.

Because honey bees learn to avoid tripping the flower, it is important to use large colonies containing a large percentage of young workers. Colonies must be distributed throughout the large field, rather than have them concentrated in one area. As mentioned previously, more efficient pollination could dramatically increase alfalfa seed production. Assume that an acre (0.4 hectare) contains about 2 billion flowers, and 200 million (10%) set seed pods, each containing 5 seeds. There are approximately 220,000 seeds per 0.453 kg (1 lb); therefore, one acre is capable of producing about 2,059 kg (4,545 lb) of alfalfa seed. Other studies have shown that 46% of the flowers are capable of setting pods when pollinated. Improving alfalfa seed production offers interesting challenges.

To illustrate another challenge, consider the almond *(Prunus amygdalus)* growers' requirements. Commercial varieties are self-sterile or self-incompatible; that is, in order to set fruit, the ovary must receive pollen from another cultivar. Normally orchards are planted in rows— two containing the main cultivar, then one pollinizer. Almonds blossom between mid-February and mid-March, and flowers are highly attractive to honey bees. The crop is machine-handled and small kernels are desired, especially for the candy trade, so the grower desires a maximum fruit set. Honey bees are the only pollinating insect capable of transferring pollen from one cultivar to the other. But at this time, the weather is unpredictable, and honey bees will not forage when the temperature is below 14°C (57°F). Also at this time the colonies are usually weak, so the grower has difficulty not only in finding strong colonies, but also in depending on proper temperature for honey bees to forage. Developing a strain of honey bees that will fly at a slightly lower temperature would be highly beneficial to the almond grower. As in alfalfa seed production, the honey bee is an important factor influencing a profitable crop. Observations suggest two or three strong colonies per acre are needed to insure a good fruit set, and colonies must be placed in small clusters throughout the orchard rather than have them concentrated in one area. About the only thing the grower can do is to rent strong colonies, place them in proper position, and hope foragers will move readily among cultivars. The entire crop is dependent on good pollination performed only by the honey bee.

Soybeans *(Glycine max)* are probably one of the most important crops grown in the United States for oil and a high quality protein meal. Introduced to the United States from Asia in the early 1800's, the soybean today includes varieties (cultivars) ranging in maturity from 80 to 200 days. The soybean always had been considered self-fertile, so little attention was given to the presence of honey bees and other pollinating insects until recently. While some beekeepers report obtaining honey from soybeans, others state that honey bees never visit soybean fields.

Production of soybeans does not meet world needs. One way to increase yields is through plant breeding and selection. As early as 1930, it was demonstrated that hybrid soybeans can outyield the average parent in amounts ranging from 6 to 117%. While these are laboratory and small plot tests, most plant breeders agree that hybrids offer a potential for increased yields and are worthy of further investigation. The honey bee would be a logical choice as the carrier of pollen.

Before a systematic breeding program can be initiated, more has to be known about the relationship between the honey bee and soybean flowers. While no recommendations are available on how to utilize honey bees in a soybean field, progress is being made in explaining why earlier reports appear contradictory. The quantity of nectar and pollen produced appears to be influenced by genetics of the plant and climatic factors. In routine breeding and plant selection programs, characteristics were not considered, overlooked, or ignored simply because the plant has a high degree of self-fertility. However, before hybrid varieties can be developed, it will be necessary to understand floral structure and behavior as well as nectar secretion. Plants will have to be made attractive to honey bees by selecting lines which produce nectar and pollen and possess flowers compatible with honey bee behavior.

McGregor (1976) lists 166 crops and 52 ornamental and wild flowers which are dependent on or greatly benefit from cross pollination with insects. While other creatures naturally pollinate some plants, the honey bee is the only insect that can be easily managed and precisely manipulated to meet the needs and interests of today's society. Replacements and substitutes have been found for honey and beeswax; however, science has not found another way to effectively and efficiently pollinate crops other than by utilizing the services of the honey bee.

BIBLIOGRAPHY

ERICKSON, E.H. 1975. Honey bees and soy beans. Am. Bee J. *115* (9) 351–353.

ERICKSON, E.H. 1975. Variability of floral characteristics influences honey bee visitations to soybean blossoms. Crop. Sci. *15*, Nov-Dec, 767–771.

MARTIN, E.C. 1975. Use of bees for crop pollination. *In* The Hive and the Honey Bee. Edited and published by Dadant and Sons, Hamilton, Ill.

MARTIN, E.C., and S.E. McGREGOR. 1973. Changing trends in insect pollination of commercial crops. Ann. Rev. Entomol. *18*, p. 207–226.

McGREGOR, S.E. 1976. Insect Pollination of Cultivated Crop Plants. U.S. Dep. Agric. Handb. 496.

13

Enemies of Honey Bees

Diseases, parasites, and predators are living organisms and nature's counteracting forces. While some view the balance of nature as highly desirable, the basis of agriculture is to protect beneficial organisms such as honey bees, and when possible, create an environment favorable to their welfare. To accurately diagnose a problem in a hive it is essential to consider the colony and its environment as one unit. Factors such as climate and crop conditions including the surrounding agricultural practices can influence its well being. Food reserves, honey as well as pollen, always should be available if it is to prosper.

Some marvel at the fact that between 30,000 and 60,000 honey bees can live in such close contact yet be subject to so few diseases. People tend to associate diseases and some parasites with crowded conditions. This phenomenon, however, is less spectacular if individual honey bees are viewed as components of one organism, the colony (p. 6).

Honey bees can be attacked by bacteria, fungi, viruses, and protozoa. Like other organisms, the honey bee has several natural systems of protection. Hive sanitation is one of its first lines of defense. Workers instinctively remove foreign objects from the hive as soon as they are discovered. While old workers normally fly out to die, those accidentally injured or crushed during hive manipulation are immediately hauled out. If a foreign object cannot be removed, it sometimes is coated with wax or propolis. It is not unusual to find a mouse so treated lying at the bottom of the hive. Spaces and holes inside the hive too small to utilize are filled or sealed with propolis, so dirt and debris which could harbor disease organisms do not accumulate. Some chemicals (terpenes) in propolis are known to be natural disinfecting agents.

Pathogenic microorganisms can be transmitted or harbored with food supply; therefore several natural defense systems evolved. Fresh pollen is highly perishable. The addition of nectar helps form the pellet, and sugar encourages growth of *Pseudomonas* bacteria which uses the oxygen within the cell. *Lactobacillus,* another bacteria, grows well in this oxygen-free environment and produces lactic acid, which acts as a preservative (p. 44).

The technique of storing pollen in the comb could act as a defense against poisonous pollen. Generally pollen from a single source (species) is stored in a single cell. It can be presumed that should a source of toxic pollen be encountered, it would be advantageous to have this material concentrated in several cells rather than be mixed with all the others. The method and manner of storing nectar (honey) also have defensive implications. The low pH, moisture content, and high osmotic pressure make it a very poor medium for bacteria, fungi, and molds to grow.

Even though the colony has several natural defenses, its members are susceptible to several pathogens. Because of the importance of honey bees, more is known about their diseases than diseases of all other insects.

DISEASES

Man undoubtedly carried honey bee disease along with the colonies as he settled in new areas. Plants and animals were transported wherever man traveled without serious thoughts of introducing pests. Changes in beekeeping technology also had their effect on the diseases. Removing the colony from the traditional skep or box and placing it in the conventional hive with reusable combs significantly increased the ease at which brood diseases could be spread. Generally, it is the healthy colony which swarms, and at one time, this was the means by which numbers of colonies were increased (p. 10). Diseased skeps were undoubtedly discarded and beeswax made into candles, effectively eliminating the disease organisms.

The most common disease of honey bees, even today, is foulbrood. It was first recognized and named in 1771, primarily because it emits a distinctive obnoxious odor. In 1882, in New York, this one disease was recognized as two separate diseases termed American and European foulbrood. Based upon descriptions in the literature, American foulbrood (AFB) was in Iowa in 1865, and was introduced into Wisconsin in 1870. The introduction into Wisconsin originated from Italy, with a shipment of Italian queens brought into south-central Wisconsin. Adam Grimm, who imported queens, died in 1876. His equipment was sold and dispersed to several locations. By 1900, 12 countries had established infestations of American foulbrood, the most distant one over 200 miles from the original site. It was reported that Adam Grimm did what he thought best to contain the disease, but his efforts were not successful. The serious nature of the disease was recognized by 1896, and in 1897 the Wisconsin State Legislature enacted an Apiary Inspection Law.

By 1914, the disease nearly eliminated the beekeeping industry, which was once the fifth largest business in the state. More stringent search and burn laws, along with intensive educational programs, were initiated and the industry recovered.

Because of the seriousness of AFB, today most states have some type of laws or regulations governing inspection, importation, and shipping of honey bees, used equipment, and honey bees on comb. Some state regulations are quite specific, others are general, allowing regulatory officials discretion in the method of controlling the disease.

All known diseases of honey bees are specific for only one stage in the life cycle, and foulbrood is restricted to early larval stages. It is a highly communicable disease, spread by healthy workers robbing diseased colonies, or by the beekeeper transferring contaminated equipment. Diseased colonies become weak, since old workers are not replaced, so they are subject to being robbed of their honey.The pathogen is carried along with the honey and thus the disease is spread. With many diseases, the owner can normally exercise some care or precaution to protect his livestock from contracting a disease. This can be done by immunization, vaccination, isolation, and/or good management. However, there is no way a conscientious beekeeper can keep his colony from contracting disease should careless neighbors live within honey bee flight range. Beekeeper education has emphasized the basic responsibility each individual has towards neighboring beekeepers. Diseased colonies should be treated or destroyed as local law may require and maintained in such a manner so other foragers do not rob honey. However, there is a danger of contracting foulbrood from "wild" colonies established in hollow trees, walls of buildings, or other sites normally inaccessible to inspection.

Foulbrood disease is easily identified and because of this, the procedure to bring it under control was quite simple, even though costly. Inspectors were trained to diagnose the disease in the field, not having to rely on expensive, confirming laboratory tests, although they were available if and when required. While there was some resistance and opposition to the search and burn procedure, inspectors had the moral support of progressive beekeepers and the backing of the law.

During the active honey bee season, a diseased colony will have several distinguishing features. By using a combination of these symptoms it can be accurately identified.

AMERICAN FOULBROOD (AFB)

The newly infected larva will begin to turn brown rather than retain its pearly white appearance. Just before death, it turns lengthwise in the cell, rather than remain coiled at the bottom. Most larvae will die after

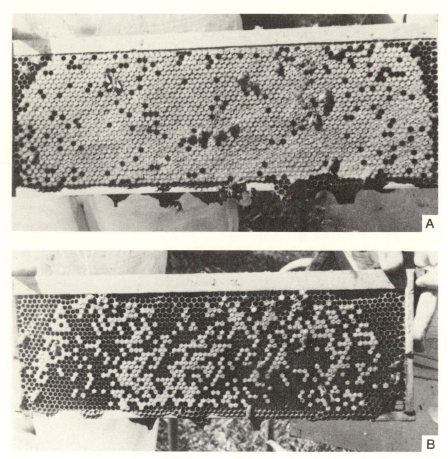

From USDA

FIG. 13.1. (A) NORMAL SEALED BROOD COMB FROM A STRONG COLONY. (B) TYPI-
CAL COMB FROM A COLONY WITH A BROOD DISEASE

the cell is capped. The cap may appear sunken or have a hole punctured
in the center. If the disease was present for some time, the brood will be
scattered throughout the comb, rather than appear in a regular, compact
pattern. Dead and dying larvae emit a characteristic odor of decaying
flesh. During this period, the larval skin is easily punctured or appears to
disintegrate. When a toothpick or match stick is inserted and with-
drawn, the contents, resembling glue, adhere to it, and will stretch out
about 2.5 cm (1 in.). The dead larva requires about one month to dry
down into a brittle scale, firmly attached to the bottom of the cell. If the
larva pupated before death, as it would if infected later in life, then a

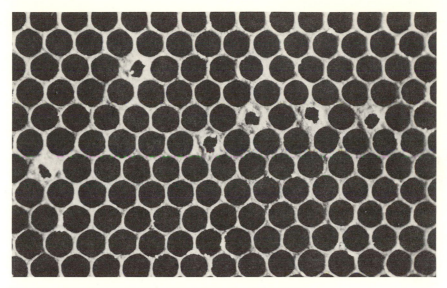

FIG. 13.2. PUNCTURED CAPS INDICATIVE OF FOULBROOD
Emerging healthy workers remove entire cap.

"tongue" protrudes from the scale to the top of the cell. The presence of a dried, brittle scale and tongue will remain in unused or abandoned equipment indefinitely and is used to ascertain whether old, used equipment is diseased. While this is not an absolute guarantee, a competent inspector can classify combs as free, suspect, or infected with disease.

The causal organism of AFB is *Bacillus larvae,* a Gram positive, spore-forming bacteria. The spores are extremely persistent, remain viable for decades, and withstand 107°C (224°F) in honey for 40 minutes. As few as 10 spores are sufficient to fatally infect a 24-hour-old larva, but as larvae mature, they are most resistant to infection. The spore germinates in an environment low in oxygen (larval gut); however, the vegetative stages grow best aerobically, that is, once it reaches the cells lining the gut. From here it rapidly invades the remaining tissue.

The exact mechanism of resistance attributed to age is unknown, but believed to be due to the fact that the vegetative forms are excreted before they penetrate the cells. The vegetative form of this bacteria is non-infective, but once the tissue is invaded the disease is fatal. Spores are formed in the decaying tissue, and the larva dies two to four days after the cell is capped.

To a small degree, resistance to AFB is genetically influenced. All young larvae are equally susceptible and old larvae are immune, but at the age of 18 hours, for example, the LD_{50} is 2,500 spores for the resistant strain

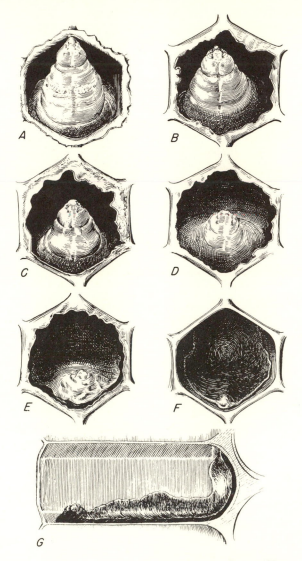

FIG. 13.3. HONEY BEE LARVAE KILLED BY AMERICAN FOULBROOD, AS SEEN IN CELLS

(A) Healthy larva at age when most of brood dies of American foulbrood. (B–F) Dead larvae in progressive stages of decomposition (remains shown in F are scale.) (G) Longitudinal view of scale.

and 1,300 for the susceptible strain. Spores apparently germinate less readily in the gut of resistant strains. Adults of the inbred resistant lines are able to detect diseased larvae and clean out the cells earlier than non-resistant lines. This early clean-out is done before spores are formed in dead tissue; therefore workers have reduced the possibility of becoming contaminated and further spreading the disease when feeding larvae.

The behavioral process of cleaning dead larvae from cells by workers is genetically controlled by two recessive characters, one for uncapping the cell and the other for removing the contents. Homozygosity for both factors is required for the greatest disease resistance. The behavior towards removing dead larvae is not specific for AFB; brood killed with cyanide gas, for example, is handled as if it died from AFB.

The factor of disease resistance has been misinterpreted by some and exploited by others, leading some people to equate resistance with immunity. Currently no commercially available lines of honey bees are immune to AFB. To verify that specific lines are more resistant than others would require elaborate and closely controlled tests or experiments.

EUROPEAN FOULBROOD (EFB)

This disease, like AFB, can also be identified by a series of characteristics without laboratory confirmation. While some beekeepers question the value or necessity of distinguishing between AFB and EFB, some state regulations require that only colonies infected with AFB be destroyed. Most larvae infected with EFB die before the cells are capped. They lose their pearly white color and appear yellowish. Larvae remain coiled at the base of the cell, look like they lose their plump appearance, begin to turn brown, and the tracheal system becomes visible. Recently dead larvae do not have the glue-like characteristic when punctured with a small stick, and remain dry as easily detachable, rubbery scales, rather than ones which are firmly attached to the base of the cells. Dead and decaying larvae emit a characteristic sour odor, rather than one of decaying flesh.

The causal organism of EFB is *Streptococcus pluton*. However, at one time it was thought that there were four other organisms involved with this disease. These other organisms are now believed to be secondary invaders. The pathogen multiplies under anaerobic conditions within the food mass inside the gut of the honey bee larva, usually killing it before the cell is sealed. Larvae infected later in life may survive and pupate, but the resulting pupae are smaller than normal. Bacteria are voided into the cell, and when other young workers clean and polish this cell they become contaminated. When they begin serving as nurse bees, young larvae are infected, and thus the disease spreads. If there are a small number of larvae in proportion to the number of adult bees, most larvae will survive an infection, but contaminate the cells. As the disease organ-

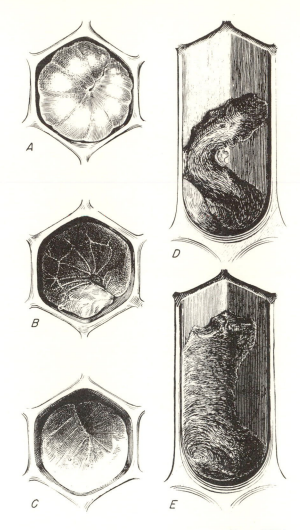

FIG. 13.4. HONEY BEE LARVAE KILLED BY EUROPEAN FOULBROOD, AS SEEN IN THE CELLS

(A) Healthy larva at earliest stage when the brood dies of European foulbrood. (B) Scale formed by a dried-down larva. (C) One of several positions of sick larvae prior to death. (D) and (E) Longitudinal views of scales from larvae that assumed a lengthwise position prior to death.

isms multiply, and as larval food becomes less abundant, large numbers of larvae will suddenly die, before the cells are sealed. Workers removing these unsealed dead larvae do not become contaminated, so the colony recovers, provided it is not robbed by others before it has an opportunity to increase in population. Because of the seriousness of foulbrood and the importance of these diseases, the U.S. Department of Agriculture and some Land Grant Universities continue to study the basic biology of these diseases. Comprehensive USDA Bulletins 780, 804, and 809 contain basic information on the biology of honey bee pathogens, and more recent findings are summarized by Gochnauer *et al.* (1975). Laboratory procedures used to diagnose honey bee diseases and parasites are summarized by Shimanuki and Cantwell (1978).

CONTROL OF FOULBROOD

There are differences of opinion with reference to the best method of controlling foulbrood, especially when economics is considered. The standard control procedure for AFB was to kill the honey bees in the evening or on a cold day, place them and all associated equipment in a hole, and burn the contents. History proved that this procedure was effective, but costly. Most beekeepers agreed with the basic philosophy of search and burn; however, some found it hard to accept destruction of an entire colony, especially if it contained a substantial quantity of honey and only a few dead larvae were found as evidence of foulbrood. There were times when the local law officer had to accompany the inspector to some bee yards.

Variations in laws and regulations exist among states. Some permit hive bodies, bottom boards, and top covers to be scorched with fire or boiled in a solution of lye, rather than be burned. These procedures reduce the incidence of disease, but also discourage or force many beekeepers out of business.

The discovery, in 1944, that larvae can be protected by sodium sulfathiazole and, later, oxytetracycline gave hope to many beekeepers. These drugs have been tested on a world-wide basis and prove beyond a doubt that they are effective in protecting larvae from foulbrood organisms.

As mentioned previously, only young larvae are susceptible to foulbrood. Introducing a small quantity of either drug into the sugar syrup or pollen supplement is enough to protect it through this critical stage. Neither drug kills spores of AFB, so any which remain in the comb or equipment are viable. The simplest way to treat a diseased colony is to mix the legal quantity of drug into the sugar syrup and feed it. Sometimes a weakened colony refuses to take sugar syrup in sufficient quantities to be of benefit. Mixing the required quantity of drug with powdered sugar and dusting the mixture over the cluster forces workers to treat themselves. In the process of cleaning and grooming, they ingest and distribute sufficient quantities to protect the developing larvae. In most cases, three separate treatments, four days apart, are adequate to revitalize the colony. Sodium sulfathiazole has been used at ½ to 1 gram (0.0175 to 0.035 oz), and oxytetracycline, 3.25 grams (0.1137 oz) mixed in 3785 ml (1 gal.) of sugar syrup per colony. Suppliers advise treating colonies four to six weeks before the honey flow, or after the crop is removed. Only oxytetracycline is effective on EFB.

At one time, there were hopes of developing a simple, economical way to sterilize combs and equipment with fumigants. Ethylene oxide has been evaluated under laboratory conditions. While it kills AFB spores and wax moth larvae, under field conditions some spores survive. Equipment needed for proper fumigation is expensive, so industry has been reluctant to invest in it.

Regulatory agencies are currently reevaluating environmental effects of chemicals used in agriculture. Because a material has been successfully used to control a problem in research trials, or the use was one legally approved, does not imply that it is currently registered. Also, state laws vary; therefore, the prudent beekeeper should always inquire of local or state regulatory agencies as to the current status of a specific drug or chemical.

There are several systems used to control diseases; each has its merits. Many commercial operators routinely treat all colonies in early spring and in late fall by adding the required amount of either drug to the sugar syrup. This system is simple; unskilled labor can be utilized to mix the drug and feed colonies. One disadvantage is that the drug is given to many healthy colonies. Another procedure is to treat only diseased colonies. Management must be more precise, as all colonies must be closely inspected and precautions taken to prevent robbing. Care must be taken to prevent equipment from diseased hives from mixing with healthy hives. The third option is to burn, as was once practiced. A variant of this system would be to salvage wax (where legal) and sell it to those interested in arts or crafts (non-honey bee users) such as candlemakers, then fumigate, boil in lye solution, or scorch the remaining wooden parts with fire.

Some states have modified or repealed search and burn laws, and rely on the integrity of regulatory officials to use judgement in determining the best, or most effective, method of control. This prompts endless discussions, debates, and arguments among individuals who remember the days before the availability of drugs. Some of these people advocate intensive inspection and burning. They reason that the hobbyist and non-professional beekeeper lack knowledge and skill to control the disease, and that they eventually will infect the commercial beekeepers. Others feel that it is too costly to maintain inspectors in the field and to destroy colonies and equipment which could have been saved by an economical drug treatment. Less than one percent of the colonies in-spected show evidence of disease. Some oppose the use of drugs on the basis that honey is a pure food and no chemicals or drugs should be used in its production. But regulatory officials and others maintain, and have data to support their opinion, that if drugs or chemicals were applied properly no honey would be contaminated. Others still have hopes that a resistant strain, or strains of honey bees, will be developed. Even though diseases of honey bees are important, the quantity of drugs used by the beekeeping industry is small in relation to developmental costs. Companies cannot justify performing necessary research to meet regulatory agency requirements. Products which are effective in con-trolling diseases of other animals, and hence a larger market, offer some hope. However, developmental costs specific to honey bees will have to be assumed by the Federal government or beekeeping industry.

SACBROOD

Honey bees are also susceptible to a virus disease, sacbrood. Even though it was recognized over 60 years ago, little is known about the disease. The incidence may range from all colonies in an apiary being infected to none; and some colonies may have only a few diseased larvae, whereas others have 90% dead brood. The exact method by which the virus is propagated and spread is not clearly understood. Under labora-tory conditions, infected young larvae, 12 to 36 hours old, show symp-toms within 48 hours after inoculation. Reliable estimates indicate that one dead larva contains sufficient virus particles to kill one million larvae, yet the disease disappears each summer and is not spread even to a healthy colony when infected combs are inserted in it. Dead larvae lose their infectivity in 3 weeks to 10 months, influenced by temperature and other unknown factors. Recent evidence suggests that the virus can be maintained and multiplied asymptomatically in adult honey bees. They probably serve as a reservoir for the disease during late summer and winter, when very few diseased larvae are noted.

The significance of the disease is that it should be distinguished from foulbrood. Sacbrood is rarely fatal to the colony, and no control is available. However, mistaking sacbrood for foulbrood can lead to serious consequences.

Larvae infected with sacbrood change from their normal pearly white appearance to a yellow, thin gray, and finally black color. The head is the first part to become black, and it usually remains in an upright position. The contents of the dead larva is watery; but the larval skin remains strong and intact, containing the contents, hence the name sacbrood. Dried down scales are easily removed from the cells, have a rough texture, and are brittle.

FUNGUS DISEASES

Chalkbrood has been reported in the United States since 1968, although some believe it might have been present earlier but not reported or identified. The causal organism is *Ascosphaera apis*. As most fungi grow best in cool and humid regions, it is not unusual that the disease is not uniformly distributed in the United States. In some regions it is found sporadically all summer, particularly after cool and damp weather. Smaller colonies, which might be a little colder, appear to have a higher incidence of this disease than larger ones. Drone larvae also seem to be more susceptible than worker larvae, possibly because they are usually on the periphery of the comb, which might be a little cooler.

Larvae are most susceptible to chalkbrood when they are four days old. Remains of dead larvae (mummies) can be found in unsealed as well as sealed cells. As the mycelium grows over, it takes on an off-white appearance, hence the name. Fungus is transmitted by workers. Undoubtedly spores are quite numerous, but they will grow only when conditions are suitable. No chemical control agents are registered to control this disease.

Stonebrood is another disease caused by a fungus belonging to the genus *Aspergillus*. While it is not very common, the dead larvae are covered with a powdery green growth. The mummies become hard and brittle, hence the name.

NOSEMA DISEASE

The most serious disease of adult honey bees is caused by *Nosema apis*, a microsporidian protozoa. It was first discovered in Germany by Zander in 1909. Fearful that this parasite would be introduced accidentally into the United States and devastate the thriving beekeeping industry, the U.S. Department of Agriculture sent representatives to Germany to study the problem. Meanwhile discussions were underway to ask for authority to restrict the importation of honey bees. However, when the first worker bee was selected to illustrate the simplicity of a diagnostic test, nosema was found. Examination of honey bees in many other parts of the country further confirmed that the disease was already present.

Infection is caused by adult honey bees ingesting spores of the parasite. They germinate after entering the ventriculus, then move into the epithelial cells. Inside the cell the parasite multiplies, usually destroying it in six to ten days. The epithelial cells are shed releasing large numbers of spores into the gut, which accumulate in the rectum. For many years, it was assumed *Nosema apis* would only affect the digestive tract; however,

TABLE 13.1. IDENTIFYING CHARACTERISTICS OF HONEY BEE BROOD DISEASES

Character	Disease			
	American foulbrood	European foulbrood	Sacbrood	Chalkbrood
Appearance of brood comb	Sealed brood Sunken, or punctured cappings	Unsealed brood Some sealed brood in advanced cases	Sealed brood Scattered cells with punctured cappings	In small colonies, often at edge of brood nest
Age of dead brood	Older sealed larvae or young pupae	Unsealed larvae	Older sealed larvae	Mature to recently sealed larvae
Color of dead brood	Dull white, becoming brown to almost black	Dull white, yellowish to brown, or almost black	Grayish brown to black	Moldy and off-white, chalky
Consistency of dead brood	Soft, sticky	Water or pasty	Watery, tough skin forms a sac	Firm pellet or mummy
Toothpick test	Sticky	Not sticky	Sac punctured	Firm mummy
Odor of dead brood	Animal glue or decaying flesh	Sour	None to slightly sour	None
Scale	Flat on lower side of cell Adheres tightly to cell wall Fine, threadlike tongue of dead pupae adheres to roof of cell	Twisted in cell, easily removed Rubbery	Head curled up Does not adhere tightly to cell wall Brittle	Removed by workers, mummies can be found on bottom board
Control treatment	Oxytetracycline Sodium sulfathiazole Burn contents Contact local regulatory officials before buying and using drugs	Oxytetracycline	None available	None available

more recent evidence indicates that they can also live in the malpighian tubule and hypopharyngeal glands. A queen can become infected in the shipping cage, if the attendants are parasitized and especially if old workers are selected.

Infected workers do not recover. During warm weather and when flight is possible, they normally leave the colony to void feces, reducing the possibility of contaminating others. But when workers are confined to the hive because of cold weather, or for example, when being shipped in a package, the comb or inside of the package is soiled and the infection spreads to others. While nosema infection does not kill honey bees outright, it does shorten life. Queens are superceded much earlier, brood rearing efficiency is reduced, and honey production suffers.

In southern regions, where workers are not confined for prolonged periods, nosema incidence is lower, symptoms not as conspicuous, and the problem is often ignored. However, confining workers in a package along with a young queen for several days stresses them. Prior to installing, the routine practice is to gorge workers with sugar syrup by spraying the entire package. Ingested along with the sugar syrup and some feces are nosema spores. Because the newly installed colony is without replacement workers for at least 21 days, colony growth is retarded and honey production is significantly lowered.

Nosema can be diagnosed by a combination of symptoms. By carefully separating the abdomen and thorax, the digestive tract is exposed. Normally the ventriculus has a straw-brown color; if infected with nosema, it is swollen and creamy white. Crushing it in a drop of water releases a large number of microscopic spores. Behavior of nosema-infected workers can sometimes be mistaken for paralysis, starvation, or insecticide poisoning. The wings may appear disjointed, abdomen distended, and the stinging reflex may be absent. On warm days, crawling workers will be noted around the front of the hive, unable to fly. Sometimes the front of the hive will be stained with feces, suggesting that workers are unable to accurately control their flight as they either leave or return to the hive.

Colony management can reduce the severity of infection. Any disruption of normal brood rearing such as lack of pollen, queenlessness, brood diseases, insecticide damage, and prolonged confinement will increase nosema incidence. Reusing equipment and combs soiled with feces, which occurs when colonies starve, also intensifies the disease.

Strong colonies appear to withstand the disease better than weak or small ones. Encouraging winter flights by providing hives with wind protection and a top auger hole entrance facing south also reduces the disease.

Nosema spores remain viable for up to 6 years when frozen, but are killed in 10 minutes in water at 57°C (135°F). At 21°C (70°F) spores

From USDA

FIG. 13.5. *(TOP)* DIGESTIVE TRACT FROM A HEALTHY BEE. NOTE THE INDIVIDUAL CIRCULAR CONSTRICTIONS ON THE VENTRICULUS. *(BOTTOM)* DIGESTIVE TRACT OF A HONEY BEE WITH NOSEMA DISEASE. NOTE THAT THE CIRCULAR CONSTRICTIONS ON THE VENTRICULUS ARE NOT CLEARLY DEFINED

remain viable for 2 months, but are killed when incubated at 35°C (95°F) in 21 days. Fermentation kills spores in about 10 days, and putrefaction between 5 and 22 days, depending on the temperature. Sunlight kills them between 15 and 51 hours, depending on circumstances. Spores remain virulent in dead workers for one week to four months, depending on temperature of the surrounding environment.

Live steam can be used to clean contaminated equipment and cages. Combs can be sterilized by precisely controlled heat treatment, or with fumigants such as ethylene oxide or acetic acid.

An antibiotic, fumigillin, first used in 1953, has proved to be very effective when used as part of a good management system. It does not kill spores, but protects workers against infection when it is in the food. Approximately 5 grams (0.18 oz) of the formulated product is suspended in 3750 ml (1 gal.) of sugar syrup and fed to a colony in the fall after brood rearing is reduced or stopped. Workers entering the winter season will receive the medication and the remaining sugar syrup will be stored in and around the brood area and used during the winter or early spring.

The disease will not be eradicated, but drastically reduced. Some bee-keepers find it profitable to add fumigillin to the sugar syrup in the spring feeding. During winter, especially in northern areas, some workers will die in the hive and soil the comb. As the colony expands, the contaminated comb is cleaned by young workers. Fumigillin fed at this time will protect them from infection.

As mentioned previously, packaged bees originating from southern regions are generally infected with nosema. The sugar syrup used to spray the package and gorge workers should contain fumigillin. The newly installed package should also be fed at least 3750 ml (1 gal.) of the sugar syrup containing fumigillin immediately after installation.

Honey bees also are affected by other bacteria, *Rickettsia,* fungi, protozoa, and mites. Currently, parasitic mites on honey bees are not found in the United States. The Honey Bee Act of 1922 apparently has been successful in preventing its introduction. It is present, however, in the Brazilian-African hybrid in South America. Viruses are known to cause two types of paralysis in honey bees. None of these pathogens are as serious to the beekeeping industry as foulbrood or nosema. Whether this will change remains to be seen.

WAX MOTHS

Experienced beekeepers readily recognize wax worms. There are two species, the lesser, *Adroia agrisella*, and the greater, *Galleria mellonella*, which is more common. Larvae are called wax worms which accurately describes their activity; that is, they are pests of combs. Like foulbrood, wax moths are found wherever honey bees are kept, and were transported inadvertently by early settlers. The greatest damage is done in warmer regions, because they are active for a longer time. They are without doubt the most destructive pests of brood comb in storage. Left alone, the larvae will tunnel throughout combs leaving a mass of webbing and debris.

A strong colony can defend itself against wax moths, but weak or diseased ones soon become victims of serious damage. Clusters of eggs are laid in dark cracks, crevices, and between hive parts, out of reach of workers. Hatching and developmental time is directly related to temperature. At 27°C (80°F) it takes about five days; at 10°C (50°F), five weeks.

Newly hatched larvae can often be found crawling between the inner and top cover and between frames. Those fortunate enough to escape the reach of workers will continue feeding on wax and other debris. Any brood comb unprotected by workers will be rapidly invaded. It is for this reason that strong colonies are not damaged, since workers will vigorously remove any larvae from the hive. Larval development proceeds at a rate proportional to the temperature ranging from one to five months. Mature larvae are about 22 mm (⅞ in.) long. The most favorable temperature for development is between 30° and 35°C (85° and 90°F) which is the normal hive temperature during the summer. Between 4° and 7°C (40° and 45°F), larvae do no feeding, essentially going dormant.

Wax worm larvae obtain nutrients from impurities in brood comb such as pollen, propolis, and cast skins of honey bee larvae. While beeswax is consumed in the process of feeding, it does not provide a complete diet. Larvae feeding on white or extracting comb do not complete development. Once growth is complete, larvae leave the area where they fed, crawl to a secluded spot, spin a cocoon, and pupate. Parts of a heavily infested hive will be covered by a mass of cocoons. Pupal development lasts between 8 and 65 days.

Adults are about 19 mm (¾ in.) long, with a wing span of 38 mm (1½ in.). Color, to a degree, is influenced by diet; the darker the brood comb, the darker the pigmentation. They usually are seen in the resting position with wings folded in a roof-like position; when disturbed, they run for a short distance before flight. After mating, the female begins depositing eggs in four to ten days, usually in clusters near the source of larval food. Adults require little or no food. They are capable of detecting established colonies from a great distance, probably by odor.

Because of its simple life cycle and behavior, the greater wax worm frequently is used in laboratories, and due to the ease at which it can be reared in confinement, large numbers are produced and sold as fish bait. Another beneficial and often overlooked function wax worms perform in nature is to help reduce foulbrood and other diseases associated with brood combs. Wax moths will find a colony established in a hollow tree or wall of a building as readily as one in a conventional hive. Should this colony become infected and die, wax worms will not prevent other workers from robbing the honey. But once it is gone, they will thoroughly destroy the infected brood comb. A new swarm taking up residence a year or two later would have to construct its own comb. While the foulbrood organisms would not be destroyed, the possibility of this new swarm being exposed to them is far less than if it would have reused the old comb.

The best defense against the wax moth is a strong colony. In southern areas the loss of a queen in fall usually means the destruction of brood comb. Keeping hives scraped clean of excess wax and propolis helps reduce the population. The greatest loss occurs when infested brood combs are placed in storage unprotected.

In northern areas, wax moths are a seasonal problem. At −6.7°C (20°F) all stages are killed in about 4 ½ hours; at −15°C (5°F), 2 hours. If brood comb is removed from the colony in late summer and early fall, significant damage can occur before the arrival of cold weather. Storing combs in warm buildings can intensify the damage. Hobbyists can pro-

TABLE 13.2. EFFECT AND INFLUENCE OF TEMPERATURE ON WAX MOTHS

| Temperature | | Effect |
°F	°C	
120	49	Death, all stages, in 40 min
115	46	Death, all stages, in 80 min
85-95	29-32	Optimal for rapid growth
75-80	24-27	Eggs hatch in 5 to 8 days
50-60	10-16	Eggs hatch in 35 days
40-45	4-7	No larval feeding or growth
20	−7	Death, all stages, 4½ hours
10	−12	Death, all stages, 3 hours
5	−15	Death, all stages, 2 hours

tect brood combs by placing them in a deep freezer overnight, then keeping them in a moth-free environment such as in tightly sealed plastic bags. Combs can also be freed of wax moths by heat treatment. However, temperature control must be precise; otherwise they will melt. Exposure at 45°C (115°F) for 1½ hours or 49°C (120°F) for 40 minutes will kill all stages of wax worms. Only combs without honey can be so treated because heat softens beeswax, and combs will sag.

Brood combs can be fumigated with ethylene dibromide (EDB), carbon dioxide (CO_2), or paradichlorobenzene (PDB). Vapors must be confined for a specific time, and temperature regulated. Naphthalene (the active ingredient in moth balls or flakes) is used interchangeably with PDB to protect furs and woolen clothing from insect damage. However, it will not protect brood combs from wax moths. As with the heat or cold treatment, fumigation does not protect combs from reinfestation, so they must be stored in a moth-free environment or moth-tight container.

Wax worms can be a serious pest on comb honey. As mentioned previously, they will not complete development on white comb but the presence of small dead larvae or evidence of their burrowing and feeding on the wax cappings of comb honey offered for sale in most areas is in violation of food sanitation laws, and repulsive to the consumer. Comb honey can be fumigated with CO_2, which is exempt from current pesticide regulations. EDB also is currently approved. Regulations change so prudent beekeepers should always consult with regulatory officials regarding current status of pesticide products.

Occasionally larvae of Mediterranean flour moths *(Ephestia)* and carpet beetles *(Dermestes)* invade brood combs in storage and feed on pollen and dead brood. Control procedures for those pests would be similar to those used for wax worms.

MAMMALIAN INTRUDERS

Mice will not damage a natural colony of honey bees; however, they probably are the most destructive mammalian pest encountered by the beekeeping industry. Workers will protect the hive from intruders during warm weather, but when clustered, mice can enter and leave at will through the bottom entrance. Being cavity dwellers, mice find the lower part of the hive a suitable nesting site. They will carry in bits of grass, leaves, rags, and comparable material. Once this is accumulated in the bottom of the hive, they are well protected from workers and can rear young unmolested, consuming dead honey bees, pollen, and honey contained in brood comb. While the cluster is not disturbed, brood comb in the lower hive body is either damaged or destroyed.

Mouse-damaged comb can be placed above the cluster in spring. As the colony expands, workers will usually reconstruct it, but build drone rather than worker cells. Most beekeepers salvage the remaining wax and install new foundation.

There are differences of opinion as how best to protect the hive from mice. Some use entrance restrictors, others install hardware cloth in front of the opening. The argument against reducing the entrance size is that it becomes plugged with ice and dead workers, thus reducing ventilation.

Protecting hive bodies in storage is less of a problem. Poison baits strategically placed under and on top of a stack of hive bodies is effective. There is always the danger of poisoning non-target animals. The active ingredient in some poison baits is closely regulated and may not be available to the hobbyist.

Mice can be easily excluded from stacked hive bodies. If they are placed on a level floor, the first two hive bodies should be free of holes or damaged edges. If the floor is uneven, inverting a telescoping top cover and using it as a base to stack hive bodies effectively excludes them. The top of the stack should be tightly covered.

Skunks eat insects, and once they acquire a taste for honey bees or learn how easy it is to obtain a meal in front of a hive, they are difficult to discourage. They usually begin by consuming guard bees on the lower entrance, then learn that by scratching on the hive body it entices others to emerge, only to be consumed. A skunk will feed for about an hour, and return night after night, eventually depleting the population. Stingers have been found in the mouth, throat, and stomach of dissected skunks, but apparently this does not discourage them.

Evidence of skunk damage can be noted by a weakened colony and scratch marks around the bottom entrance. Colonies preyed upon are more defensive, and difficult to manipulate. Skunks are fur-bearing animals and in many states protected by statute, but some allow live trapping and even killing of a destructive animal. Appropriate regulatory agencies should be contacted before such action is taken.

Trade journals on occasion publish ingenious devices or techniques on how to discourage skunks and other mammalian pests. Electrically charged wires or fences have been effectively used by some. Driving a series of nails through a board and placing it at the front entrance is purported to work. Apparently the skunk is unable to sit or rest comfortably on the exposed nails and goes elsewhere.

Marauding bears can be extremely destructive, destroying a hive more thoroughly than vandals. While the total number of hives destroyed by bears is not large, a beekeeper encountering a bear usually loses the honey bees and all the combs.

It is well established that bears will tear up ant hills, rotting logs, and stumps in search of insects, and one fortunate enough to come upon a hollow tree or log used as a hive would have a feast. Some believe bears evolved as natural predators of honey bees since no other mammal in the northern hemisphere can so accurately detect a colony and destroy a hive with so little impunity. Euro-asian bears have been reported to be heard "bawling with pain from stings around the muzzle," but continued to feast on honey and brood comb. Stingers do not provide adequate protection against bears. Whether they have a natural "sweet tooth" is conjecture. There are those who contend that animals which rely on ripe fruit as a part of the diet enjoy eating sweets. Man and bears fit into this category. However, most observers report that bears appear to prefer brood and brood comb over honey.

Bears are omnivorous, creatures with a poorly developed sense of sight and sound, but an acute sense of smell. There are reports that they are able to detect a hive from a great distance. Hunters have used old brood comb to bait bears to a specific location during hunting season. While the practice is highly controversial among hunters, some states outlawed it on the basis of honey bee diseases. Some unscrupulous or ignorant beekeepers might sell their diseased brood combs for such purposes, greatly increasing the possibilities of further spreading the disease.

After tipping a hive, the raiding bear carries the brood chamber several meters (yards) from the site. Most of the displaced workers will return and hover at the original location of their hive, while the bear breaks apart frames and eats the comb, honey, brood, and pollen with less harassment.

It is quite difficult to protect an apiary from bears. Hobbyists have placed several hives on top of flat roof buildings. Installing an electrically charged fence is of little value unless a ground wire such as poultry netting is placed flat around it. The bear's feet are such that they provide a poor contact with the ground. Forcing it to stand on the grounded poultry netting corrects the problem.

Trapping, shooting, or poisoning in most states is either controlled or illegal. Some states reimburse citizens suffering damage from protected animals; others do not. Therefore, before decisions are made, local authorities should be contacted.

A unique partnership of preying on honey bees evolved between a bird and mammal in Africa. A bird, the honey guide *(Indicator indicator)*, is not able to break into the normal hive. It is one of the few animals able to digest beeswax, as its intestine harbors specific microorganisms. At one time it was believed that the honey guide actually directed or "guided" an African predator, the honey badger *(Mellivora capensis)*, to a bee tree. The current belief is that the honey guide simply follows the honey badger. When it opens a hive, exposing comb, the honey guide is able to feed on comb, wax, and honey, along with the honey badger.

In addition to the described pests, many other animals and microorganisms feed or live on honey bees. Some may inflict a loss to the beekeepers, but not others. For example, a dragon fly or swallow may, by chance, capture a queen, drone, or worker in flight. Loss of the latter two would be inconsequential. Losses attributed to the non-selective feeders such as some birds, robber and dragon flies, frogs, toads, and spiders, in general, are not measurable.

BIBLIOGRAPHY

ANON. 1918. Biennial Report, Apiary Inspection. Wisconsin Dep. Agric. p. 67-74.

GOCHNAUER, T.A., B. FURGALA, and H. SHIMANUKI. 1975. Diseases and enemies of the honey bee. *In* The Hive and the Honey Bee. Edited and published by Dadant and Sons, Hamilton, Ill.

HOAGE, T.R., and W.C. ROTHENBULLER. 1966. Larval honey bee response to various doses of *Bacillus larvae* spores. J. Econ. Entomol. *59* (1) 42-45.

MOELLER, F.E. 1978. Nosema disease—Its control in honey bee colonies. U.S. Dep. Agric. Tech. Bull. *1569.*

SHIMANUKI, H. 1973. Identification and control of honey bee diseases. U.S. Dep. Agric. Bull. *2255.*

SHIMANUKI, H., and G.E. CANTWELL. 1978. Diagnosis of honey bee diseases, parasites, and pests. U.S. Dep. Agric. ARS-NE 87.

STURTEVANT, A.P. 1920. A study of the behavior of bees in colonies affected by European foulbrood. U.S. Dep. Agric. Bull. *804.*

USDA. 1972. Controlling the greater wax moth. U.S. Dep. Agric. Bull. *2217.*

WHITE, G.F. 1919. Nosema disease. U.S. Dep. Agric. Bull. *780.*

WHITE, G.F. 1920. American foulbrood. U.S. Dep. Agric. Bull. *809.*

14

Problems and Challenges
Confronting the Beekeeper

FARM CHEMICALS

Over 400 chemicals made into several thousand formulations or products are used in agriculture. In addition to insecticides, these include fungicides, herbicides, growth regulators, hormones, fertilizers, rodenticides, and minor and trace elements. It is estimated that about 20% are highly toxic to honey bees, 15% might be classed as moderately toxic, and the majority (65%) are harmless. However, many toxic ones rarely or seldom come in contact with honey bees. For example, cabbage must be routinely protected from worms, but sprays do not affect the beekeeper.

That insecticides are toxic to honey bees and damaging to the colony should not be surprising, because chemicals cannot distinguish between harmful and beneficial insects. It is man's use or misuse that causes problems. One of the more challenging issues facing the beekeeping industry is the use of insecticides in agriculture. While this is not a new problem, no simple solution is in sight.

In order to kill, the insecticide must enter the organism's body and disrupt a vital process. Most insecticides enter by penetrating the exoskeleton or by ingestion with food or water, damaging the nervous system. Chlorinated hydrocarbons, phosphates, and carbamates have unique penetrating powers. Some penetrate the exoskeleton quickly; others must be ingested before they are toxic. Honey bees can be killed by either or both methods. Inorganic insecticides such as the arsenicals must be consumed in order to be toxic. The use of arsenicals, lead, and chlorinated hydrocarbons has largely been discontinued or outlawed because of low demand, objectionable residues, or their adverse effect on non-target organisms.

The insecticide problem in relation to honey bees began about 1870 when fruit growers began spraying apple and pear trees with Paris green to control codling moth. The earliest verified honey bee poisoning incident occurred on pears in 1881, and by 1890 to 1900 many others observed similar incidents. By 1904, there were reports that honey bees were killed also when cover crops underneath fruit trees were contaminated by sprays applied to trees. In 1917, a molasses bran, Paris green bait, was perported to kill honey bees. By 1920, well-planned tests were performed to determine the toxicity of some insecticides to honey bees. Aircraft applications began in 1926, adding further to the problem of poisoning. Most of the poisoning cases occurred when plants were sprayed during blossom time. Honey bees ingested run-off spray mixtures in water accumulating on leaves or in ruts and depressions in the field. Some of these problems were solved by better management of the spray programs.

MODERN AGRICULTURE

Changes in American agriculture are described on p. 121. Agricultural chemical usage greatly expanded during the late 1940's and 1950's. This, along with larger, more efficient machines capable of treating massive acreages in a relatively short time, added new dimensions to beekeeper problems. Some weeds which produce excellent honey and pollen were either reduced or eliminated from fence rows, ditch banks, and wasteland. Selective herbicides used on cropland further reduced some highly desirable plants used by honey bees. Examples of a few are mustard, yellow rocket, thistle, and smartweed *(Polygonum)*. So the honey bee not only faces some highly toxic chemicals, but has fewer plants from which to gather nectar and/or pollen.

Some modern agricultural practices are not always in the best interest of the beekeeper, especially those interested in honey production. Alfalfa, for example, yields an abundant, excellent quality, light-colored honey. Grown as a livestock forage, its value is in the high protein content which declines as the crop matures. In temperate regions the standard practice was to harvest alfalfa at full bloom. This was a compromise among winter hardiness, resistance to root diseases, and maximum yield of protein and total digestible nutrients per acre. New varieties which are disease resistant and have a greater degree of winter hardiness permit harvest at about 1/10 bloom (first flower). While this practice increases the protein yield, the beekeeper is deprived of valuable nectar source.

Changes in some agricultural technologies now require insecticides, where previously none were needed. Peas were cut, and then hauled to a central location for shelling, then canning or freezing. Worms that might have been on the vine were either dislodged, or left the crop before processing. Peas are now cut and shelled in one operation in the field, and only edible portions are hauled to the processing plant. However, fields so

TABLE 14.1. CHEMICAL COMPOSITION OF ALFALFA FORAGE AT FOUR STAGES OF MATURITY

Constituent		Pre-bud	Bud to Mid-bud	First Flower to 1/10 Bloom	Near Full Bloom
		EXPERIMENT A			
IVDDM[1]	%	67.7	61.4	56.0	53.0
Nitrate (NO_3)	%	0.11	0.07	0.04	0.06
Crude Protein	%	26.5	23.3	17.9	15.8
Crude Fiber	%	21.0	27.9	34.0	35.4
Cellulose	%	24.8	30.5	34.6	36.2
Ether Extract (Fat)	%	1.8	1.5	1.5	1.4
Total Ash	%	11.5	8.7	8.8	7.8
Calcium	%	1.48	1.47	1.41	1.28
Phosphorus	%	0.40	0.34	0.28	0.24
Potassium	%	2.16	1.61	1.42	1.10
Iron	ppm	310	184	154	153
Manganese	ppm	58	50	52	46
Copper	ppm	7.8	6.8	5.8	6.0
Cobalt	ppm	0.11	0.09	0.10	0.09
Zinc	ppm	31	29	23	24
Carotene[2]	ppm	228	224	208	105
pH of Tissue[2]		5.58	5.46	5.65	5.50
		EXPERIMENT B			
TNC[3]	%	15.7	13.6	11.1	13.3
Starch	%	4.8	6.8	6.0	6.2
Sucrose	%	5.6	2.7	2.4	2.7
Glucose	%	2.6	2.1	1.3	2.1
Fructose	%	2.7	2.0	1.4	2.3
		EXPERIMENT C			
Crude Protein	%	28.60	23.69	17.90	15.31
Alanine	%	1.28	1.07	0.80	0.81
Arginine	%	1.27	0.94	0.78	0.74
Aspartic Acid	%	3.28	—	1.85	1.88
Glutamic Acid	%	2.20	2.07	1.42	1.53
Glycine	%	1.14	0.94	0.76	0.77
Histidine	%	0.55	0.42	0.37	0.35
Isoleucine	%	1.07	0.88	0.69	0.68
Leucine	%	1.82	1.53	1.20	1.17
Lysine	%	1.41	1.10	0.90	0.87
Methionine	%	0.40	0.30	0.21	0.22
Phenylalanine	%	1.19	0.93	0.81	0.75
Proline	%	1.00	0.89	0.75	0.69
Serine	%	1.08	0.86	0.74	0.71
Threonine	%	1.20	—	0.78	0.61
Tyrosine	%	0.82	0.62	0.54	0.51
Valine	%	1.35	1.08	0.97	0.86
		EXPERIMENT D			
Total-N	%	4.54	3.21	2.89	2.08
Protein-N	%	3.11	2.38	2.13	1.56
Non-protein-N	%	1.43	0.84	0.76	0.52
Ammonium-N	%	0.009	0.007	0.006	0.004
Nitrate-N	%	0.053	0.034	0.016	0.013
Free a-amino-N	%	0.243	0.194	0.137	0.103
Asparagine-N	%	0.178	0.148	0.110	0.089

Table 14.1. *(Continued)*

Constituent		Pre-bud	Bud to Mid-bud	First Flower to 1/10 Bloom	Near Full Bloom
Glutamine-N	%	0.009	0.006	0.006	0.004

Source: From Rohweder and Smith (1975).
[1] *In vitro* digestible dry matter.
[2] Analyses on fresh tissue.
[3] Total nonstructural carbohydrates.

harvested must be worm-free; otherwise, fragments find their way into the finished product. The processor would be in violation of Pure Food and Drug laws if the finished product contained insect fragments exceeding the official tolerances. Even without the law, the consumer would find insect fragments in food to be repulsive and would not purchase the product.

In some situations there is no reason to apply an insecticide to a crop in bloom. For example, some fruit trees blossom for a short time, and damaging insects can be controlled by treatments before or after. In other situations, the solution is not as simple. Seed alfalfa and cotton are examples of crops that are attractive to honey bees over a long period. If the application is delayed or omitted, the farmer will lose production.

Timing of the spray application can reduce the hazard to honey bees. Quick-acting, short-residual insecticides applied at night are sometimes effective. Some plants are attractive at a specific time. Corn, for example, is attractive in the mornings—so afternoon and evening sprays are less damaging to nearby colonies.

REGULATIONS

The manufacture, sale, and application of insecticides are closely regulated under the Federal Insecticide, Fungicide, and Rodenticide Act (FIFRA) enacted in 1947. It was further amended as the Federal Environmental Pesticide Control Act in 1972, 1975, and 1978. It requires that all products intended for sale must be registered with the Environmental Protection Agency (EPA). Before registration is granted, the manufacturer must submit test results showing that the product is: (1) effective against the pest, (2) will not injure people, animals, crops, or the environment, and (3) will not leave an illegal residue on the food or feed. The manufacturer must provide directions for use, which includes mixing, application, and associated safety precautions. FIFRA also allows local and state regulatory agencies to impose additional restrictions on the use of any product.

Labels on some products prohibit application during blossom time. Others state that an application made to blooming plants may be harmful to honey bees, but does not specifically prohibit its use. Therefore, a farmer can legally protect the crop without regard to honey bees, provided the label does not specifically prohibit its use. But some states may require farmers to obtain a local permit from a regulatory official before using some products. The permit can be denied if, in the opinion of the regulatory official, the crop is highly attractive to honey bees, and there is a commercial apiary within flight range. Other times the permit may require the applicator to notify nearby beekeepers of his intention to spray, and it is up to the beekeeper to take appropriate precautions. Commercial beekeepers in some areas try to avoid placing hives near crops which require routine or frequent insecticide treatments. For an example of specific local regulations, see Mussen (1978).

HONEY BEE KILLS

Colonies can be killed easily if they are accidently, inadvertently, or through ignorance sprayed with an insecticide. But a colony has several behavioral traits which help guard against massive poisoning from the field. As mentioned previously (p. 44), old workers forage for nectar and pollen. While any worker killed in the line of duty represents a loss to the colony, losing an old worker is not as damaging as losing a young worker. Foraging workers poisoned in the field seldom return to the hive. Even those contacted with a slow-acting insecticide tend to become disoriented and get lost; even if they did return, the guard workers probably would not admit them because of a "foreign" odor.

A spray to one field may not be disastrous to a colony, but seldom is only one field in an area treated. So a colony may lose its foragers in field A on Monday, in field B on Wednesday, and in field C on Friday. The end result is a seriously weakened colony.

A far more serious type of poisoning occurs when pollen is contaminated with an insecticide like carbaryl. It is a relatively safe product because of its poor penetrating characteristics, but a very effective insecticide especially when ingested by insects. Honey bees continue to gather pollen from treated fields in routine fashion. They are not affected by the spray, but workers in the hive who eat the contaminated pollen are killed. Instead of losing one old worker out in the field, the colony now may lose several to possibly a hundred young ones in the hive. In serious poisonings, a large number of workers accumulate around and inside the hive. If the queen survives, she usually stops laying, and unsealed brood starves since there are not enough workers to feed them.

The relationship between corn and honey bees is unique. It is a wind-pollinated plant, and under normal circumstances honey bees will visit it only if no other source of pollen is available. The crop can be safely sprayed when other more attractive plants are blooming or if the spray is directed at the ear, rather than over the entire plant. Corn produces pollen in the morning; generally, afternoon spray applications have been less damaging.

CONFLICTS

Conflicts sometimes arise between beekeepers and corn growers. Most sweet corn must be protected from corn ear worm and sometimes corn borers. Applications must also be timed precisely so that the chemical kills the larvae before it penetrates the stalk or ear. Sweet corn for processing usually is grown in concentrated areas near processing factories. The flight pattern of one apiary may be over two to five different farmers who grow corn under contract for competing processing companies. Each field may have a different maturation date, hence require a different treatment schedule. Some farmers apply their own insecticide, but many hire custom applicators who use either aircraft or ground machines. Losses can be reduced if ground equipment is used and the spray is directed at the ears. However, there are times when ground equipment cannot be used because of rains or wet fields. Wind may delay application for a time, so aircraft have to be used to "catch up." Under such circumstances, beekeepers can expect losses if honey bees were foraging on corn.

The beekeeper can take precautions in limited situations by covering or moving hives. However, the same hive may have workers in several fields because of differential plantings, so they may have to be covered several times a week which is impractical.

The most serious, and often highly emotional, conflicts arise between the part-time and/or hobby beekeeper, and custom applicators in heavily settled areas. In some areas there are a large number of hobby beekeepers, and honey bees are very important to them. Assuming the flight range of 1.3 km (2 miles), one custom applicator may be applying insecticide over the flight range of 3 to 10 or more hobbyist beekeepers. To expect a custom applicator to notify each beekeeper of his intention to spray is unreasonable, as one hobbyist may be out of town for a week, another on vacation, and another may work nights, or one hobbyist may be notified by several applicators of intentions to spray within a one- or two-week period.

ENCAPSULATION

As mentioned previously, some insecticides have unique penetrating powers, being nearly as toxic to organisms (and man) on the skin as if ingested. Some insecticides hydrolyze (react with water) rapidly and the end results are a number of harmless materials. It is for this reason that some potent insecticides can be applied to food crops. After a waiting period of a specific number of days, the sprayed crop is free of the insecticide and safe to eat.

A technique of encapsulation has been discovered and patented. In theory, the process is simple. Divide the chemical into very small particles and coat each one with a non-toxic substance such as plastic or gelatin. This process solves two problems associated with insecticides. It reduces the hazard associated with highly toxic, rapidly penetrating substances, and it controls the rate of hydrolysis. A highly poisonous substance like methyl parathion has been made 6 to 12 times less toxic to people than conventional methyl parathion. However, when encapsulated methyl parathion is applied to corn it behaves somewhat like carbaryl. It is carried into the hive on pollen, and the end result is similar—numerous dead honey bees. Conventional methyl parathion normally would kill only the field workers, damaging the colony less severely.

TO REDUCE LOSSES

In some instances, farmers and custom applicators can help reduce colony losses by choice of product. The University of California classifies products into highly, moderately, or slightly toxic categories. But a highly toxic product may have a short residual life, so a highly toxic substance, in some circumstances, may be safely used, and other times it may be highly detrimental to nearby colonies. Formulations known to be hazardous might be avoided, even though they are more economical. For example, dusts, as a rule, are more hazardous to honey bees than are liquid sprays. Special circumstances related to the crop should be taken into consideration. Carbaryl is a safe product, but highly hazardous when applied to corn because it can be carried to the hive on pollen. In this case more hazardous products such as diazinon or parathion might be substituted. Workers in the field will be killed, but the colony will be spared. Sometimes it is necessary to incorporate other management techniques into the total program. If the cover crop in an orchard is visited by honey bees and it is necessary to spray trees, mowing or discing the crop may reduce or eliminate the problem. Pesticide use decisions should be made on a professional basis, taking all the interrelated factors into consideration.

Beekeepers can take precautions to reduce losses also. When small numbers of colonies are involved, confining the workers for one or several days is possible, provided precautions are taken to prevent overheating. Adding an extra empty hive body which provides more space or covering the colony with wet burlap will help keep the colony cool. Replacing the top cover with a wire screen might help prevent overheating. Those engaged in pollination services would be in a position to move from the immediate area.

Perhaps more is written and reported on the insecticide-honey bee problem than on any other subject involving honey bees. Some groups and individuals advocate outlawing, banning, or severely restricting specific insecticides regardless of consequences to other segments of the agricultural economy. Still others totally disregard the rights of the hobby beekeeper, insisting that honey bees are trespassers and should suffer the consequences unless they are specifically brought in for pollination. As mentioned previously, this is not a new problem, and conflicts of interest are seldom resolved to the complete satisfaction of the involved parties. Those beekeepers residing in a heavily agricultural area which have crops that need to be protected to meet modern standards of quality food will have to accept the fact that on occasion colonies may be injured. The insecticide user will be confronted with more stringent regulations, which tend to restrict his choices, and those not able to comply will be forced out of business.

INDEMNITY PROGRAM

The Agricultural Act of 1970 authorized the federal government to indemnify beekeepers who, through no fault of their own, suffered a loss of honey bees when a properly registered product was applied to nearby crops. The county Agricultural Stabilization and Conservation Service (ASCS) administers the program. The beekeeper with assistance from or under direction of a local apiary inspector or ASCS personnel submits evidence of loss. These might be: signed statements by certain disinterested people, inspection reports, tax returns, or any other evidence to the satisfaction of the local ASCS to substantiate losses. Colonies are classified as destroyed or severely or moderately damaged, and payment is based on severity of loss. Congress can renew or cancel the program, depending on its collective judgement.

Users and/or applicators of highly toxic pesticides generally are held liable for any damages if the product is misused or carelessly applied, or if it drifts over to another area. Unused material and empty containers must be disposed of properly. Should a colony be injured by such acts, the ASCS would not reimburse a beekeeper but would have to recover damages by court action.

AFRICAN-BRAZILIAN HONEY BEES

That agricultural production can be dramatically increased by introducing new "stock," "blood," or "genes" into a population has been known for generations. Many of our high-producing domesticated plants and animals are products of imports and/or crosses with them. The U.S. Department of Agriculture financed importation of queen honey bees as early as 1860. Old beekeeping journals contain numerous reports of queens shipped from Africa to Europe and North America. As with many popularized articles even today, the search for and introduction of new organisms are well reported, but the success or failures of these undertakings are seldom mentioned. So it is unknown whether any of these early imports survived. However, there are several reports of successful introductions into England and France of honey bees believed to have their origin from the area around Mount Kilimanjaro. One English writer in South Africa wrote that the African honey bees are "not the sweetest-tempered of bees, but with good management repay their owner," and offered to send some home (presumably to England). Africa at one time was thought to have 5 distinct races separated by geographic barriers; however, today 10 or 12 are believed to exist. It was assumed that many of these African races were not dramatically different from those the Europeans described (p. 5), and hence not studied in great detail.

It was logical that Brazilians would look to Africa for genetic material to improve their stock, originally derived from Italians. In 1956, a geneticist, W. E. Kerr at the University at São Paulo, went to Africa for some queens. Of the 133 *Apis mellifera adansonii* selected, 47 survived—1 from Tabora, Tanzania and 46 from Pretoria. They were established in an apiary in São Paulo in November, 1956. From this group, Kerr selected 35 which he thought most promising, and transferred them to an apiary near a eucalyptus forest near Rio Claro. He intended to get hybrids through the use of instrument insemination. These would be used for further research and breeding, eventually releasing productive stock to the industry. He used all the necessary and standardized precautions of confining queens to the hives. However, a visitor saw his hives and noticed piles of pollen in front, and removed the queen excluders. Before the tragic mistake was noted, 26 colonies swarmed.

Once on the loose, these *adansonii* spread rapidly by swarming and interbred or hybridized with the native population, forming the "Africanized bees" which soon replaced the Brazilians derived from Italian stock.

The Africanized honey bee dramatically affected beekeeping in Brazil. In the southern area, a number of hobby beekeepers simply went out of business as the reports stated that they were "more interested in keeping honey bees than producing honey." But the more progressive commercial beekeepers, using standardized equipment, now claim to produce 1.2 to 2 times more honey than previously. In northern Brazil where conditions are more primitive, things were different. A swarm settling in villages and even a metropolitan area often created havoc. Sometimes the incidents were over-dramatized. However, honey production records speak for themselves. To 1970, no excess honey was produced for export from Recife, Pernambuco, but in 1972, 800 tons were exported to Liverpool, England.

Because of publicity, study teams and journalists began traveling to Brazil to observe the problem. As would be expected, widely differing reports were issued, and journalists coined the name "Killer Bee," which the public, unfortunately, now equates with the Africanized hybrid. This honey bee was dramatized in television documentaries, movies, and popularized magazine articles. Unfortunately, some writers do not always separate imagination from facts.

In 1970, a study team sponsored by the National Academy of Science-National Research Council conducted a three-week field study and issued their report in 1972. In summary, their recommendations were to:

(1) Study behavior and biology of the African (adansonii) and Africanized hybrid
(2) Strengthen or establish quarantines to prevent introductions
(3) Develop a method to positively identify this hybrid
(4) Screen germ plasm for lines useful for stock improvement
(5) Explore possible barriers to confine the further spread of the established population

They also reported that populations which dispersed south from São Paulo to the more temperate regions were more manageable than those which moved north. Whether this is due to climate or to selection pressure is unknown. It is assumed that beekeepers naturally eliminate the more aggressive colonies.

The Brazilian government imported Italian queens and encouraged beekeepers to place additional drone combs in their European-stocked hives with the hopes of diluting the African influence; however, most beekeepers failed to cooperate and some actually were opposed to the program because they feared a loss in honey production.

Parts of Africa were settled by English who imported European honey bees. Some postulated that they interbred with native races, but such apparently was not the case. As in Brazil, the adansonii replaces European stock. The amount of true hybridization which occurs is unknown or difficult to measure.

The African honey bees evolved in the tropical and more hostile environment than the so-called European races, and this undoubtedly influenced their behavior. To objectively measure defensiveness, a leather ball 20 mm (0.8 in.) in diameter, stuffed with cotton, is exposed for one minute, 50 mm (2 in.) from the entrance. By recording the number of stings per unit of time, rather precise comparisons can be made among colonies. For example, a highly defensive colony will inflict about 1.5 stings per unit of time on the test ball, whereas a gentle one will inflict 0.01 stings per unit—a 150-fold difference. Geneticists believe that defensiveness is controlled by possibly eleven pairs of genes, as determined by a series of standardized genetic crosses and backcrosses.

As mentioned previously (p. 53), defensiveness is also under the influence of pheromones, a highly complex mixture of chemicals. The Africanized strain has about five times more 2-heptanone and one-third more isoamyl acetate than Italians, but the venom is apparently the same. Africanized honey bees respond more vigorously to vibrations and movement, and it is not unusual to have several nearby colonies or an entire yard become agitated at one time. *Adansonii* will, on the average, sting a person as far as 144 meters (480 ft) from the hive; the Africanized, 35 meters (114 ft); and Italians, 19 meters (63 ft). When hives are intentionally disturbed, *adansonii* become agitated in 22 seconds; Africanized in 30 seconds; and Italians in 43 seconds.

Based on what is known about European honey bees, some of the reports from Brazil and Africa regarding behavior were difficult to believe. However, as more information became available, some of the stories were surprisingly accurate.

Initial reports on rapid movement or dispersal of the Africanized honey bee were difficult to understand. European honey bees reproduce, spread, or migrate quite slowly. A healthy colony in temperate areas normally swarms about once a year, and in tropical regions possibly every three or four months, if food is available. The average swarm will travel from 1.6 km (1 mile) to 5 km (3.1 miles). In tropical highlands, they were known to spread 14 km (8.4 miles) per year. Based on these observations, it is possible to predict the rate of spread. But the Africanized honey bee spread or advanced rapidly, moving as far as 320 km (192 miles) per year, in other areas 500 km (300 miles), and, over a 5-year average, it moved 80 km (48 miles) per year. Some believed that the Brazilian beekeepers helped spread them by traveling to the area around São Paulo to capture wild swarms which they added to their apiary or asked colleagues and fellow beekeepers to send them some of this new blood.

The rapid spread of the Africanized honey bee cannot be fully explained; however, the frequency of swarming partly relates to the rapid movement. A healthy colony will swarm about once every 48 to 50 days. Swarms also will travel a considerable distance. They have been found on an island 20 km (12 miles) off the coast of French Guinea and were known to land on boats 10 km (6 miles) offshore. It is estimated that a swarm can fly 10 to 50 km (6 to 30 miles) between resting sites. The mechanism by which a swarm making such long distance flights replenishes its energy is unknown. Assuming that a swarm travels 19 to 24 km per hour (11 to 15 mph), it should have enough energy for a 45- to 90-minute flight and travel 14 to 36 km (8.4 to 21 miles).

The Africanized honey bee has a unique adaptation of absconding; that is, when food is short, the entire colony leaves the hive and searches for a new location, presumably near food. However, Europeans will often starve under the same conditions. Some of the "unprovoked" attacks on man or animals reported in the press are believed to be a reproductive or absconding swarm simply landing on the individual or animal just like a European honey bee sometimes settles on a branch of a tree or shrub. Absconding swarms are not necessarily gentle, so a person could receive a few stings. Even if a gentle swarm settled on a person not familiar with honey bees, this person would be horrified and naturally attempt to escape or dislodge them and get stung.

The Africanized honey bee has developed the ability to utilize practically any kind of cavity as a hive, whereas the Europeans are rather selective in the choice as described on p. 50. They will use termite nests, old tires, mail boxes, space under steps to houses, holes in rocks, and frequently out in the open in a sheltered area. Compared to Europeans, thermo regulation is poor; they cannot survive low temperatures. This adaptation is compatible with a tropical environment. Swarms have been known to land near an established European colony, and the swarming Africanized queen enters and replaces the established queen. To prevent this from happening, the entrance can be covered with queen excluder material.

The *adansonii* in Africa is now being studied more seriously. It, too, has some unique adaptations. Because of the large amount of predation, mating flights are short. In controlled experiments, European queens usually disappeared on mating flights, whereas *adansonii* returned quickly, suggesting a very short flight or an abundant and widely dispersed supply of drones. *Adansonii* are efficient foragers, and for this reason Kerr was correct in looking to this race for breeding stock. It makes shorter, more frequent trips; therefore, recruitment within the hive is greater. It flies at a lower temperature (p. 44), later in the evening, and at a lower light intensity. Even in a very light rain, if nectar is available, they have been observed foraging at 3:30 AM and as late as 10:30 PM on moonlit nights. Their defensiveness is documented, and so-called "attacks" on people and animals are known to occur to the extent that in some areas of Africa such incidents do not make the newspapers.

Some have expressed concern and even fear that the Africanized honey bee will eventually enter the United States and destroy the part-time and hobby beekeeping industry. Based on what is known, regarding winter survival, most knowledgeable people agree that permanent establishment would be possible in a small part of the southern United States. Colonies will survive short intervals with temperatures as low as –10°C (14°F) and possibly 6 to 8 weeks in areas of 10°C (50°F). While this eliminates a large area of the United States, many packages and queens are produced in areas which can sustain the Africanized honey bee. Obviously that industry would be dramatically affected by the "Killer Bee."

BIBLIOGRAPHY

ANON. 1972. Final report of committee on African honey bee. Nat. Acad. Sci., Washington, D.C.

ATKINS, E.L. 1975. Injury to honey bees by poisonings. *In* The Hive and the Honey Bee. Edited and published by Dadant and Sons, Hamilton, Ill.

ATKINS, E.L., E.A. GREYWOOD, and R.L. MacDONALD. 1973. Toxicity of pesticides and other agricultural chemicals to honey bees. Ext. Ser. Rep. M16, Univ. of California, Riverside.

FLETCHER, D.J.C. 1978. The African bee, *Apis mellifera adansonii* in Africa. Ann. Rev. Entomol. *23*, p. 151–171.

JOHANSEN, C. 1977. Pesticides and pollinators. Ann. Rev. Entomol. *22*, p. 177–192.

LEVIN, M.D. 1974. Hybridization of honey bees in South America. Bull. Entomol. Soc. Am. *20* (4) 294–296.

MICHENER, C.D. 1975. The Brazilian bee problem. Ann. Rev. Entomol. *20*, p. 399–416.

MORSE, R.A. *et al.* 1973. Early introductions to African bees into Europe and the New World. Bee World *54* (2) 57–60.

MUSSEN, E.C. 1978. Honey bees and pesticides—general guidelines for beekeepers establishing or operating apiaries in California. Am. Bee. J. *118*, p. 794–795.

ROHWEDER, D., and D. SMITH. 1975. When it comes to protein, nothing beats alfalfa. Univ. Wisconsin Ext. Circ. A 2539, Madison.

SHAW, F.R. 1941. Bee poisoning: a review of the more important literature. J. Econ. Entomol. *34* (1) 16–21.

TAYLOR, O.R. 1977. The past and possible future spread of the Africanized honey bee in the Americas. Bee World *58* (1) 19–30.

TAYLOR, O.R., and M.D. LEVIN. 1978. Observations on Africanized honey bees reported to South and Central American government agencies. Bull. Entomol. Soc. Am. *24* (4) 412–414.

15

Honey

A DISTINGUISHED HISTORY

It was undoubtedly honey which first attracted man to the honey bee. The oldest record interpreted as a man harvesting honey was found in Spain, dated about 7000 B.C. It depicts a man using a ladder to reach a hive, carrying a container to hold combs, and workers buzzing around his head. A painting at a later date in Africa shows a man doing essentially the same thing, but using smoke to pacify and repel them.

Several anthropologists have described primitive tribes gathering honey; some use smoke, and many risk their lives by climbing out on projecting rock ledges over deep ravines. Individuals of some tribes routinely mark or otherwise identify the hive or hollow tree, and it appears to be the only thing that many tribes do not own in common.

Honey played an important role in the spiritual, social, and economic life of ancient Egyptians. Carvings in temples and sarcophagi are interpreted to indicate that honey was of great national importance. Papyri refer to the medicinal value of honey, and most medicines contained milk, wine, and some honey. Egyptians drank considerable beer made of wheat, barley, and honey, as wine was not plentiful. Hebrew literature describes the promised land as a place flowing with milk and honey. Honey is referred to in the Bible and Dead Sea Scrolls, but beekeeping is not.

The Greeks believed that honey abolished fatigue, so athletes drank a mixture of honey and water before major events. Old age was attributed to fatigue and the liberal use of honey delayed its onset. At the time of Nero, honey production was a viable industry throughout southern Europe. In central and northern Europe, the forests contained many "Bee trees." During the middle ages, ownership of these was established by the discoverer cutting marks of some type in them, and this "property" was then protected by law. Ownership was often transferred by wills to monasteries. In these areas, honey was recognized as the "elixir of life" and some miraculous attributes credited to honey can be traced to these regions. It is now believed that malnutrition was common, especially in winter, because of unbalanced diets and food shortages. Those fortunate enough to eat some honey felt rejuvenated at least temporarily. The benefits might have been in part imaginary, but understandable in light of today's knowledge.

Honey also was used in surgery and burn therapy by ancient physicians long before bacteria, fungi, and molds were known to exist. Based on today's understanding of infections, some claims for miraculous cures have some basis in fact. Because of its low moisture, high osmotic pressure, and low pH, honey inhibits and, in some cases, stops the growth of microorganisms known to cause infections. The viscosity of honey provided a good, essentially sterile, protective cover over the wound and, because of its water solubility, could be removed easily. Physicians who used this kind of treatment were convinced that it had miraculous healing powers.

Even today, there are those who believe that honey is a natural food with impeccable virtues and will readily testify to its value not only as a source of carbohydrates and a sweetener, but as a cure and preventative for many ailments. But from the scientific viewpoint, it is important to distinguish between what is believed to be true based on unsubstantiated opinions, traditions, and folklore, and what is known to be true based on accurate observations and controlled experiments. This chapter describes the known characteristics and properties of honey beginning with the raw materials, through the regulations designed to assure the public of a high quality, wholesome product.

RAW MATERIALS: NECTAR AND HONEYDEW

Nectar

All life depends on photosynthesis, a chemical process which uses carbon dioxide and water to build simple sugars, which are the primary ingredients in nectar. While the process occurs in all green plants, it is only in the flowering ones where a close relationship exists between them and some insects. These insects use nectar as a source of energy, and the plants benefit by cross-pollination. Nectar is a secretion of specialized glands called nectaries, located in or near the flower (floral) area, or on any aboveground (extrafloral) structure. The basic function and structure appear to be identical, whether the gland is floral or extrafloral. Nectaries obtain their "secretions" from phloem sap, and the consensus of opinion is that they are involved in regulating osmotic pressure, allowing excess sugars to escape or be excreted from the vascular system.

During periods of rapid growth, sugars are utilized, but as certain parts complete development, nectaries excrete surplus sugars in the form of nectar. Physiological studies indicate that nectaries have a high rate of respiration, which suggests that nectar secretion is an active process. Excretory or export glands in plants are not unusual. Plants growing in alkaline areas have glands which excrete excess salts, and carnivorous plants secrete digestive enzymes which degradate the victim. Extrafloral nectaries are considered to be more primitive and are associated only with sugar excretion. Some produce a nectar of higher sugar content than floral and tend to detract pollinating insects. However, through the process of natural selection, most nectaries are located in the flowers.

Nectar secretion is a highly complex process. The quantity of nectar and sugar content appears to be correlated with photosynthesis, sugar transport, respiration, and growth. Sugar contained in nectaries appears to be synthesized in leaves closest to nectaries, except in woody plants where it is derived from stored carbohydrates, sometimes influenced by climatic and growing conditions of the previous season. There are substantial differences in nectar production among lines, clones, and cultivars of plants, undoubtedly involving hereditary factors. Differences exist in nectar secretion among plant species, age of the flower, and even the time of the day. Some flowers produce nectar only in the morning, others in the afternoon, and still others all day. Environmental factors such as relative humidity, solar radiation, air temperature, soil moisture, and fertility are also correlated to nectar secretion.

Nectar contains a mixture of several sugars plus other materials such as mineral salts, compounds of nitrogen, aromatic substances, vitamins, and a variety of plant pigments. Present also are materials which inhibit pollen germination, and some substances known to be toxic to man and honey bees. The total sugar content ranges between 5% and 80%. The ratio of sugars varies with the plant species. Some produce nectar almost exclusively of sucrose, others a mixture of glucose, fructose, and sucrose, and still others with very little or no sucrose. The quantity of honey that could be produced from a given area of land would be determined by the number of flowers (nectaries) per hectare (acre), the quantity of sugars, and length of time a plant secretes nectar.

Honeydew

A substantial quantity of honey is made from honeydew, an excretion of plant-sucking aphids, coccids, and scale insects. Those which feed directly from phloem sap produce the most abundant honeydew. The alimentary canal on these insects has a unique modification. There is a special chamber which is attached to the fore and hind gut so some liquid ingested by the insect can bypass the midgut where most of the digestion occurs. Honeydew that is excreted does not pass through the digestive system of the producing insect. Honeydew is excreted in small droplets containing between 5% and 18% dry matter. While it has not undergone digestion, the composition differs from phloem sap. Some of the carbohydrates are converted by salivary enzymes, which are added by the plant-sucking insect, and nitrogen-containing compounds are altered by microorganisms. As many as 22 different amino acids and amides have been identified, some not known to occur in the host plant, which suggests synthesis. Carbohydrates comprise 90 to 95% of the dry matter in honeydew, and the insect can sometimes be identified by the spectrum of sugar.

Manna, of Biblical fame, is secreted by a coccid, *Trabutina mannipara*, feeding on tamarisk in the Sinai; it contains 55% cane sugar, 25% invert sugar, and 19% dextrins. Honeydew composition can greatly affect honey yields because some sugars are not attractive to honey bees.

The intimate relationship between honey bees and flowering plants is often interpreted as mutually beneficial. However, another logical interpretation is possible. Honey bees are opportunists, ready to exploit any available source of nectar and pollen for their own welfare. Some plants which produce abundant nectar and pollen are wind-pollinated. Some plants also produce pollen and nectar which are poisonous to honey bees, and the honey toxic to man.

CHARACTERISTICS AND COMPOSITION

The technique used by honey bees to gather and store nectar in combs for future use is described on p. 45. After nectar is deposited in cells, moisture is evaporated and invertase changes sucrose to glucose and fructose. Invertase and other enzymes originate from the honey bee, and those found in honeydew are derived from the insect which produced it. Honey bees take a highly perishable, thin, sweet liquid, and transform it into a stable, high density, viscous, acid, high-energy food. Because of its low pH, high osmotic pressure, and low moisture, microorganisms responsible for spoilage do not grow in it.

Natural moisture in honey is what remains after the ripening process is complete. The amount will vary depending on the origin of nectar and weather conditions and range between 15 and 25%. Moisture has a profound effect on physical properties of honey such as granulation, fermentations, viscosity, and specific gravity. At 17.4% moisture it is in equilibrium with 58% relative humidity of the surrounding atmosphere, so honey can gain or lose moisture from the surrounding environment.

Complex sugars found in nectar appear and then disappear from honey

TABLE 15.1. SUMMARY OF PHYSICAL AND CHEMICAL PROPERTIES OF
EXTRACTED (LIQUID) HONEY OF AVERAGE COMPOSITION

Principal Components	Percent	Grams
Water (natural moisture)	17.2	78.0
Levulose (d-fructose; fruit sugar)	38.19	173.2
Dextrose (d-glucose; grape sugar)	31.28	141.9
Sucrose	1.31	5.9
Maltose and other reducing disaccharides	7.31	33.2
Higher sugars	1.50	6.8
Total sugars	79.59	361.0
Acids	0.57	2.6
Proteins	0.26	1.2
Ash	0.17	0.8
Subtotal	97.79	443.6
Minor Constituents	2.21	10.0
TOTAL	100.0	453.6

Specific Gravity = 1.4225
   3785 ml (1 gal.) weighs 5357 grams (11 lb 13.2 oz).
   0.453 kg (1 lb) has volume of 3.189 ml (10.78 fl oz).

Caloric Value
   0.453 kg (1 lb) = 1380 calories.
   100 grams = 303 calories.

Thermal Characteristics
   Specific heat 0.54 at 20°C (68°F).
   Conductivity at 21°C 12.7 × 10^{-4} cal/cm sec C°.
   Conductivity at 49°C 13.6 × 10^{-4} cal/cm sec C°.

Sweetening Power and sugar equivalent
   1 volume of honey equivalent to about 1.67 volume of granulated sugar.
   0.453 kg (1 lb) equivalent to about 430 grams (0.95 lb) sugar.
   3785 ml (1 gal.) contains approximately 4.25 kg (9 ⅜ lb) total sugars.

Source: Adapted from White, Riethof, Subers, and Kushnir (1962).

during the ripening process. Honey invertase is somewhat different than what is found in yeasts and molds. While the spectrum of sugars found in honey can, to a limited degree, be correlated with nectar and known enzymatic reactions, some sugars and properties of honey cannot be explained. The origin and role of organic acids are not fully understood, but they may be responsible for reactions among nectar, pollen, and other components. Carbohydrates and their significance in honey are described on p. 58.

Honey also contains traces of proteins, probably derived from honey bees, and varying amounts of acetic, butyric, citric, formic, gluconic, lactic, malic, pyroglutamic, phosphoric, and succinic acids. The acidity (low pH) is masked by sugars. The ash content ranges from 0.02 to 1%. Generally, dark honey and that derived from honeydew have a higher mineral content. Of the salts present, the concentration of potassium is highest, in dark as well as in light-colored honey. While the list of vitamins identified is impressive, the quantities are of such magnitude that they are nutritionally insignificant to humans. Through the years, researchers and analytical chemists have identified dextrins, colloids, enzymes, and other biologically active components, including some materials known to be toxic to people (Table 6.2).

One undesirable characteristic of honey is its sticky or viscous nature. This makes it difficult to handle as it adheres to containers and measuring instruments. This is often given as a reason why establishments such as restaurants, bakeries, and even homes are reluctant to use it. Warming honey to about 30°C (86°F) reduces viscosity, so it is easier to mix or transfer.

A process for drying honey was patented by Shookhoff in 1957. The moisture is reduced to 4 or 5% by a spray dry method at low temperature. The dried product is sticky and hygroscopic so it is mixed with 10% pre-gelatinized starch, heated to about 49°C (120°F) and ground to desired fineness. The resulting product is a free-flowing powder. The hygroscopic nature of honey makes it a useful ingredient in products where "freshness" needs to be retained such as in some candies, bakery goods, and tobacco products.

Color, aroma, and flavor of honey are to a degree interrelated. While color can be objectively and precisely measured, aroma and flavor are subjective judgements, yet very important characteristics for the consumer. Many desirable flavors are of local significance and may be unacceptable in another area. Buckwheat and basswood honey in one region may command a premium price, yet in another area may not be marketable. Honey which people may find unacceptable is often reserved for honey bees.

Based on the complex nature of honey, with its multitude of complex compounds, vitamins, minerals, and other components, it is understandable why no one succeeded in blending a synthetic honey based on known constituents. Neither is it surprising to expect flavor, aroma, and color to be affected by excessive heat, improper handling, and storage since aroma is in part determined by volatile substances.

Well ripened honey fluoresces under ultraviolet light, and like many organic materials, it is optically active. The plane of polarization in a beam of polarized light passed through honey derived from nectar will rotate to the left (levorotatory), and that made from honeydew, to the right (dextrorotatory). The direction and amount of optical rotation can be used in honey analysis, but more precise analytical procedures are now available.

GRANULATION

Honey is a supersaturated solution of sugars which is basically unstable, and under some conditions, such as when seeded with microscopic "seed" crystals or even dust particles, the excess sugars crystallize. Glucose crystallizes from solution in concentrations ranging between 30 and 70% depending on temperature, while fructose will crystallize only in concentrations between 78 and 95%. The tendency of honey to crystallize is related to composition, storage conditions, and preparation. Small crystals usually are associated with unheated or raw honey or with what has been seeded with fine crystals. It is often sold as spun or creamed honey. When heated honey recrystallizes, usually large hard ones form, and these require a higher temperature to redissolve. Crystallization can be predicted, but not precisely. Generally, more glucose and lower moisture content increase the tendency to crystallize. Storage temperature is closely associated with crystallization. It is most rapid at 14°C (57°F). Honey stored at −18°C (0°F) or lower remains liquid; apparently the viscosity reduces the diffusion necessary for crystals to form.

To reduce the tendency to crystallize, honey is routinely heated for 30 minutes at 60° to 66°C (140° to 150°F); lower temperatures are not effective because the microscopic crystals are not dissolved. Some commercial processors heat it to 77°C (170°F), then rapidly cool it to at least room temperature. Processors with a closed system are able to avoid recontamination with microscopic dust, or even microscopic glucose particles floating in the air.

FERMENTATION

Two fundamental reactions in the living world are photosynthesis and fermentation. The former manufactures sugars from carbon dioxide and water, and the latter recycles it back to the original components. Fermentation in honey is caused by sugar-tolerant yeasts which can be found on flowers, in soil, and on combs used the previous season, which were placed in storage without allowing workers to clean them. The first breakdown products in fermentation are ethyl alcohol and carbon dioxide. Alcohol can undergo another reaction and become acetic acid, an ingredient in vinegar, giving partially fermented honey an objectionable odor and a sour taste. Under normal conditions, honey with more than 83% sugars will not ferment. However, being hygroscopic, it could absorb moisture from the atmosphere when kept in open containers and exposed to a humid atmosphere.

Granulation will also increase the tendency of honey to ferment. As crystals form and grow, the moisture content of the remaining liquid portion increases. If yeast spores are present, moisture content increases sufficiently, and if the temperature is above 10°C (50°F), fermentation will begin. To prevent fermentation, honey can be pasteurized by heating it

FIG. 15.1. HONEY: VARYING DEGREES OF GRANULATION

to kill the yeast cells. Two factors are involved: temperature and time. For example, heating it to 63°C (145°F) for 8 minutes or 57°C (135°F) for 60 minutes or 52°C (125°F) for 8 hours will prevent fermentation.

Changes which occur in honey during storage are complex and not fully understood. Honey tends to darken with age, and if heated, the glucose disappears faster than the fructose, and the acidity increases. Storage changes can be reduced greatly if honey is held at 10°C (50°F) or lower.

COMB HONEY

Most people think of honey as a liquid product extracted from combs; however, at one time most honey was sold in the comb. With the availability of simple extracting equipment and a desire to increase production efficiency and prepare food in a form convenient for the customer, the industry shifted towards extracted honey. But there is still a demand for a limited amount of comb honey.

There are differences of opinion as to the merits and values of using comb honey. Connoisseurs of honey claim that during extraction, heating, and straining, some delicate aroma and flavors are lost, and only by purchasing comb honey are those fine qualities retained. In years past, it was not unusual for unscrupulous individuals to adulterate honey with sugar-syrup and water. The only way to be certain of obtaining pure honey was to purchase it in the comb. But with today's sophisticated laboratory equipment, regulatory agencies can readily identify an adulterated product, and most consumers have confidence that the information stated on the label is true.

Regardless of the reasons for producing and/or buying comb honey, some people gladly pay a premium price for the attractively packaged product, and some beekeepers gladly spend the extra time and effort necessary to produce it.

Three kinds of comb honey currently are sold: (1) section comb—honey is stored by workers in specially prepared boxes or containers inside the hive; (2) cut comb—honey is stored in conventional frames; the finished comb is cut into convenient portions and sold in transparent plastic boxes; and (3) chunk—honey is handled similarly to cut comb, but placed in a wide-mouth jar, and it is filled to a predetermined weight with extracted honey. In all three types, a specially prepared thin, light-colored foundation is installed in the frame.

Section comb honey is produced in standardized equipment with some slight modifications. Four small basswood boxes, $10.8 \times 10.8 \times 4.76$ cm ($4\frac{1}{4} \times 4\frac{1}{4} \times 1\frac{7}{8}$ in.) with appropriate slits, are designed to fit around one single sheet of foundation 10.4×43.1 cm ($4\frac{1}{8} \times 17$ in.). Seven of these fit in the standard comb honey super which is 12.2 cm ($4^{13}/_{16}$ in.) deep. Cleats, separators, and springs are used to position the boxes and foundation into proper location within the hive body. The top surfaces of the boxes are covered with melted paraffin or masking tape. This prevents workers from staining the surfaces with pollen, propolis, and dirt as they travel about the hive. Many producers of section comb honey have their own unique system of installing containers or boxes for comb honey.

The systems used to produce cut comb and chunk honey are identical. Standard frames are used to hold comb honey foundation. Some beekeepers use nine frames in the conventional ten-frame hive body. The reason is that normally the outside surface on each side is not filled when ten frames are used. Placing nine frames and a special board on each side will prevent workers from building bridge comb between widely spaced frames. The extra board on each side allows for conventional spacing.

Producing fine, attractive comb honey is an art. The person has to understand the behavior of a colony—to know exactly when to install the comb honey equipment, and when and how to manipulate the hive bodies to assure complete and rapid filling and capping of the cells. If empty supers are placed on the hive too soon, workers will chew the foundation. If the sealed honey is not removed immediately, workers will tend to stain the wax cappings. Normally, comb honey producers keep the colony crowded; therefore they must be on the lookout for swarming. Highest quality comb honey is produced in areas where the honey flow begins on a predictable date, nectar flow is of fairly long duration, and honey is of uniform color. While comb honey with alternating shades of different colored honey is wholesome, the average consumer prefers a uniform product.

The value of comb honey is determined to a large degree by its appearance, so careful handling is essential. Wax moth larvae can disfigure the cappings easily, so provisions must be made to either fumigate the product with approved and effective materials or place them in a deep freezer. Further details on this problem are explained on p. 142. In humid regions, additional moisture should be removed from the sections to prevent fermentation. This can be done by placing combs in a warm room with a dehumidifier. Masking tape and/or paraffin covering the boxes and any other foreign material should be removed. Suppliers sell polyethylene bags or window boxes in which the finished section is sold. Care must be taken not to pack any section with broken caps or cells. Honey dripping from a section in the store or in the consumer's home is very irritating.

Handling chunk and cut comb honey is somewhat simpler. The combs are cut to the desired sizes with a hot, sharp knife and cells along the cut edge are allowed to drain before the sections are placed in containers or bottles. Pasteurized extracted honey, cooled to about 49°C (120°F), should be used to fill the containers of chunk honey, and care should be exercised to not incorporate air bubbles around the comb.

Comb honey will crystallize; while it is still wholesome, most consumers are reluctant to buy it in this state. So shelves in the market place should not be overstocked. Some replace the crystallized stock with fresh material. Crystallized comb honey can be melted, separated from wax, and sold as extracted honey. It is possible to reliquify comb honey if precisely controlled temperature chambers are available. Heating the honey to 63°C (145°F) will dissolve the crystals, but not melt the wax. However, this temperature is very near the melting point of beeswax. Too high a temperature will melt the wax and destroy the comb honey.

REGULATIONS

Honey sold in interstate commerce is subject to federal regulations, while that which is marketed within a state is under jurisdiction of state or local regulations. The Federal Food and Drug Administration (FDA) is responsible for insuring that all food is safe, prepared and stored in sanitary conditions, and conforms to agreed-upon standards of identity and composition. It also can issue advisory opinions to interested industries. Honey for legal purposes is defined as the following. (1) Honey is the nectar and saccharine exudations of plants, gathered, modified, and stored in the comb by honey bees (*Apis mellifera* and *A. dorsata*). Honey is levorotatory and contains not more than 25% water, not more than

0.25% ash, and not more than 8% sucrose. (2) Comb honey is honey contained in cells of comb. (3) Extracted honey is honey which has been separated from the uncrushed comb by centrifugal force or gravity. (4) Strained honey is honey removed from the crushed comb by straining or other means. Unless the product meets these standards it cannot be called *honey*.

The U.S. Department of Agriculture has established color designations and grade standards for extracted and comb honey. They are designed to serve as a simple and convenient basis for establishing a quality control program and can be used as a standard by regulatory officials. Honey does not have to be graded, but most states require that such products be clearly marked or identified as ungraded when offered for sale. Not only must the honey meet certain criteria, but the containers and labels have to conform to specific standards. Copies of the federal law and information pertaining to packaging and labeling may be obtained from the Food and Drug Administration, U.S. Department of Health, Education, and Welfare, Washington, D.C., 20201.

Color is not a factor in determining quality of honey, but is important in marketing, especially when large quantities are involved. Honey is classified into seven color categories, ranging from water white to dark amber. Two methods of objectively measuring or designating color are available. A sample is placed in a small clear bottle and color is matched to permanent glass color standards, developed by the U.S. Department of Agriculture. In the other method, referred to as the Pfund color grader, a wedge-shaped glass container is filled with honey and color matched with colored glass wedge. The matching area on the wedge is measured, in millimeters, and it gives a color rating for the sample.

Honey can be classified into four U.S. grades ranging from A to D. Grade A or US Fancy must possess a good flavor of the predominant floral source, or when blended, a good flavor of the blend of floral sources, free from defects and relatively clear. Flavor means that the honey should be free from any objectionable or foreign odor caused by fermentation, carmelization, smoke, or other causes. Defects might be such items as particles of comb, propolis, and other materials which may be in suspension or deposited as sediment in the container. To be free of defects, honey should be strained through a No. 80 sieve at a temperature higher than 54°C (130°F). Clarity is in reference to air bubbles, suspended pollen grains, and other items which might pass through the sieve. A point system of assigning a maximum value of 50 for flavor, 40 for defect, and 10 for clarity is used to score honey. To meet US Grade A, the combined score must be 90 points or higher, and the honey must contain not less than 81.4% soluble solids. These may be determined with a refractometer, by specific gravity or percentage of moisture, or any other method which gives equivalent results.

To be classified as US Grade B, honey must contain not less than 81.4% soluble solids, and score at least 80 points, when scored as described above. However, if flavor score falls between 40 and 44, it shall not be graded above B, regardless of total score. US Grade C must contain not lower than 70 points. If flavor score is between 35 and 39, it shall not be graded above C, regardless of the total score. US Grade D, or substandard, is honey which fails to meet US Grade C, but still meets the legal definition of honey. The U.S. standards for grades of comb honey have been established. Considerable emphasis is placed on appearance of the comb and cappings. For example, to qualify for US Fancy, the comb must have no uncapped cells except in the row which is attached to the section box. The comb must not project beyond the edge of the section and not have dry holes. The cappings must be uniform and even in appearance, except in the row where it is attached to the section. The honey must be uniform in color, free of granulation or honeydew, and not have an objectionable odor. The requirements for US No. 1 and No. 2, while less stringent than for US Fancy, are still concerned with the appearance of the comb, its attachment to the section, and uniformity of the cappings. Copies of U.S. Standards for grades of extracted and comb honey can be obtained from the Agricultural Marketing Service, U.S. Department of Agriculture, Washington, D.C.

SELLING AND USING HONEY

The hobbyist with several hives usually is able to sell the surplus honey to friends, acquaintances, and neighbors, either directly or through a local store. It is estimated that up to 50% of the honey for home consumption is sold in this manner. Larger operators sell it to bottlers (packers) who sometimes segregate honeys from different floral sources, than are able to obtain a premium price for specific kinds. The gift package honey market has grown rapidly and is a highly profitable business when adequately promoted. Local marketing cooperatives have been formed to sell honey produced by specific groups; some have been successful, others have not. One cooperative, Sioux Honey Association, has grown to a respected national business with assets of over $25 million, marketing over 24.06 million kg (53 million pounds) of honey in 1977.

Honey consumption in the United States is relatively low, less than 1 kg (2.2 lb) per capita. Families that eat honey often use substantial quantities, yet most use very little or none. Today many youngsters reach school age without having tasted honey. The chief competitors of honey are sugars and corn syrups. Cane sugar has been known since antiquity, but was not widely distributed until more recent times. Beet sugar came into prominence about 1850 and the two, for practical purposes, replaced honey as a sweetener. The per capita consumption of sugar dramatically increased over the years. In 1700 it was about 1.8 kg (4 lb), by the Revolutionary War it had risen to 6.8 kg (15 lb), by the Civil War, 22.6 kg (50 lb), and today it is about 61 kg (135 lb). About one-third is used directly as sugar, the remainder in prepared foods. Honey was the first animal-derived product which had to face competition from cheaper plant-produced products. Others which later faced or are facing the same problem are silk, wool, butter, milk, and cheese.

There are many who feel that honey with its "natural purity," distinctive flavor, and other undefined qualities or attributes cannot be replaced. Established uses lie in many fields, including confectionary, preserves, spreads, syrups, meat packing, tobacco, and cosmetics. Some products made with honey have demonstrable differences from those containing sugars, others not. Some merchandisers rely on the name "honey" to help sell a specific product. Most products made with honey have very limited patentability, which tends to discourage innovative developments by entrepreneurs. Some products which could have sales appeal encounter technical difficulties. For example, honey ice cream would be marketable, but the freezing point is lower, so standard ice cream freezers cannot handle it. Honey jellies have never become popular because the flavors are masked by fruits, so they do not sell well. Peanut butter blends have been made, but finished products have a short shelf-life.

Most honey is sold for home table use where it serves as a spread on bread, biscuits, or crackers, to sweeten fruits, drinks, and cereals, and also for home-baked cakes, cookies, and tortes. Candies made with honey predate written history; however, due to the price of cane and beet sugar this market has been lost. More recent competitors are corn glucose and high fructose syrups.

Honey has always been associated with Middle Eastern and European foods. Migrants usually take their traditions and recipes with them, and today many ethnic Slavic, Italian, Greek, Spanish, and French bakeries continue to use honey rather than sugar when preparing certain products. Many cookbooks contain suggestions on how to substitute honey for sugar in conventional recipes, and some honey producer associations publish cookbooks containing only recipes which utilize honey.

The tobacco industry relies on honey not only as a natural sweetener for chewing tobacco and snuff, but the hygroscopic nature of honey keeps smoking tobacco from burning too rapidly. Since recorded history, honey has been valued for its medicinal qualities. While these claims are recognized for their historical interest, honey today is incorporated as part of the carrier or vehicle in some syrups and also as a binding agent in some pills. Many highly specialized uses of honey are reported from time to time. Some are closely guarded secrets such as in curing meats, and others are of historical interest such as in cosmetics and lotions.

Honey probably provided man with the first fermented product, mead. It contained the only source of concentrated fermentable sugars in quantity, even before fruits and grains became available. The exact method by which mead was first produced is supposition. As a hunter, man sometimes found an abundant supply of honey, and at other times it was scarce. Rather than abandon what could not be eaten immediately, he undoubtedly took some along in makeshift containers for future use. Some probably fermented, so rather than discard it he discovered that this fermented product could be safely consumed.

Earliest writings in central and northern Europe mention mead and suggest that it was a rather popular beverage. Oldest recipes give directions, which are quite accurate, describing how to make a fine product based on what is known today. They suggest boiling the honey-hops-water mixture, then adding some ale-yeast, spice, and herbs, some believe to mask faulty fermentation should it occur and to serve as a yeast nutrient.

Mead declined as a drink in the 1700's and 1800's possibly for several reasons. As the population expanded, honey shortages occurred, or the price increased to where the general population could not afford this luxury. About the same time, it is believed that wines became increasingly popular because of the expansion of grape production. The quality of mead was highly variable and no one was able to account for these differences until Louis Pasteur, in 1866, discovered the significance of yeast cells and their effect on fermentation.

Yeasts, generally present in or on honey, belong to the genus *Zygosaccharomyces* which grows only in concentrated sugar solutions. When the sugar solution (honey) is diluted to less than 50%, *Zygosaccharomyces* does not grow, but many other microorganisms thrive.

The usual procedure in mead production is to dilute honey with water, then either kill or suppress the undesirable microorganisms, and then innoculate the culture with saccomycetes and add a yeast nutrient such as diammonium phosphate. Honeys vary considerably in their fermentability. Generally the light ones require more nutrients than the dark honeys. As with many foods evaluated with the palate, what one finds to be highly inspiring, others may feel to be totally without imagination and character.

BIBLIOGRAPHY

ANON. 1955. Official Methods of Analysis. 8th edition. Association of Official Agricultural Chemists. Washington, D.C.

BRICE, B.A., A. TURNER, JR., and J.W. WHITE, JR. 1956. Glass color standards for extracted honey. Assoc. Off. Agric. Chem. J. *39*, p. 919−936.

CRANE, E. 1975. Honey: A Comprehensive Survey. Crane, Russak & Company, New York.

SHOOKHOFF, M.W. 1957. Process for preparing free flowing sugar powder. U.S. Patent No. 2818356. Dec. 31.

WHITE, J.W., JR., M.H. RIETHOF, M.H. SUBERS, and I. KUSHNIR. 1962. Composition of American honeys. U.S. Dep. Agric. Tech. Bull. *1261.*

Glossary of Commonly Used Terms in Beekeeping

Abdomen: Segmented posterior part of bee containing honey stomach, intestines, reproductive organs, and sting.

American foulbrood (AFB): Contagious disease of larvae caused by *Bacillus larvae.*

Antennae: Slender jointed feelers, bearing certain sense organs, on head of insects.

Apiarist: Beekeeper.

Apiary: Group of honey bee colonies.

Apiculture: Science of beekeeping.

Apis: Genus to which honey bees belong.

Apis dorsata: Scientific name for giant bee of India; largest of all honey bees.

Artificial cell cup: *See* Cell cup.

Artificial insemination: Instrumental impregnation of confined queen bee with sperm.

Bacillus larvae: Bacterial organism causing American foulbrood.

Balling a queen: Clustering around unacceptable queen by worker bees to form a tight ball; usually queen dies or is killed in this way.

Bee blower: A portable machine that produces large volumes of rapidly moving air to blow bees from combs.

Bee bread: Stored pollen in comb.

Bee dance: Movement of bee on comb as means of communication; usually same movement is repeated over and over.

Bee escape: Device to let bees pass in only one direction; usually inserted between combs of honey and brood nest when removal of bees from honey is desired.

Bee louse: Relatively harmless insect that gets on honey bees, but larvae can damage honeycomb; scientific name is *Braula coeca.*

Bee metamorphosis: Stages in development of honey bee from egg to adult.

Bee moth: *See* Wax moth.

Bee paralysis: Condition of bee, sometimes caused by virus, that prevents it from flying or performing other functions normally.

Bee plants: Vegetation visited by bees for nectar and pollen.

Bee space: A 63 to 95 mm (¼ to ⅜ in.) space through which a bee can move freely; the space between the frames and exterior parts of a hive. Bees will not build comb in it or seal it with propolis, thereby allowing the frames to be removed easily.

Bee tree: Hollow tree in which bees live.

Bee veil: Screen or net worn over head and face for protection from bee stings.

Bee venom: Poison injected by bee sting.

Bee yard: *See* Apiary.

Beehive: Domicile prepared for colony of honey bees.

Beeswax: Wax secreted from glands on underside of bee abdomen; molded to form honeycomb and can be melted into solid block.

Benzaldehyde: A liquid used to drive bees from honeycombs; a component of oil of bitter almond.

Bottom board: Floor of beehive.

Brace comb: Section of comb built between and attached to other combs.

Brood: Immature or developing stages of bees; includes eggs, larvae (unsealed brood), and pupae (sealed brood).

Brood chamber: Section of hive in which brood is reared and food may be stored.

Brood comb: Wax comb from brood chamber of hive containing brood.

Brood nest: Area of hive where bees are densely clustered and brood is reared.

Brood rearing: Raising bees.

Bumble bee: Large bee in genus *Bombus.*

Burr comb: Comb built out from wood frame or comb, but usually unattached on one end.

Butyric anhydride: A liquid used to drive bees from honey combs. It has an odor unpleasant for humans similar to that found in rancid butter and perspiration.

Cap: Covering of cell.

Capped brood: *See* sealed brood.

Capped honey: Honey stored in sealed cells.

Carniolan bee: Gentle grayish-black bee originally from Carniolan Mountains in or near Austria.

Caucasian bee: Gentle black bee originally from Caucasus area of Russia; noted for its heavy propolizing characteristic.

Cell: Single unit of space in comb in which honey is stored or bee can be raised.

Cell cup: Queen cell base and part of sides; artificial cell cups are about as wide as deep.

Chilled brood: Immature stages in life of bee that have been exposed to cold too long.

Chunk comb honey: Type of honey pack in which piece of honeycomb is placed in container of liquid honey or wrapped "dry" in plastic container.

Clarified honey: Honey that has been heated, then filtered to remove all wax or other particles.

Cleansing flight: Flight bees take after days of confinement, during which they void their feces.

Clipped queen: Queen whose wing (or wings) has been clipped for identification purposes.

Cluster: Collection of bees in colony gathered into limited area.

Colony: Social community of several thousand worker bees, usually containing queen with or without drones.

Comb: *See* Honeycomb.

Comb foundation: Thin sheet of beeswax impressed by mill to form bases of cells.

Comb honey: Edible comb containing honey; usually all cells are filled with honey and sealed by bees with beeswax.

Commercial beekeeper: One who operates sufficiently large number of colonies so that his entire time is devoted to beekeeping.

Crystallization: *See* Granulated honey.

Cut-comb honey: Comb honey cut into appropriate sizes and packed in plastic.

Demaree: Method of swarm control, by which queen is separated from most of brood; devised by man of that name.

Dequeen: Remove queen from colony.

Dextrose: Also known as glucose; one of principal sugars of honey.

Diastase: Enzyme that aids in converting starch to sugar.

Division board: Flat board used to separate two colonies or colony into two parts.

Division board feeder: Feeder to hold syrup; usually size of frame in hive.

Drawn comb: Foundation covered with completed cells.

Drifting bees: Tendency of bees to shift from their own colony to adjacent ones.

Drone: Male bee.

Drone brood: Area of brood in hive consisting of drone larvae or pupae.

Drone comb: Comb having cells measuring about four to the inch and in which drones are reared.

Drone egg: Unfertilized egg.

Drone layer: Queen that lays only infertile eggs.

Dwindling: Rapid or unusual depletion of hive population.

Dysentery: Unusual watery discharge of bee feces, often associated with nosema disease.

Emerging brood: Young bees first coming out of their cells.

Entrance feeder: A wooden runway that fits into the hive entrance so that bees may obtain syrup from a jar inverted into it.

Escape board: Board with one or more bee escapes on it to permit bees to pass one way.

Ethylene dibromide: A liquid used to fumigate honey combs for control of wax moth.

European foulbrood: Infectious disease of larval brood, caused by *Streptococcus pluton.*

Excluder: *See* Queen excluder.

Extracted honey: Honey extracted from comb.

Extractor: Machine that rotates honeycombs at sufficient speed to remove honey from them.

Feces: Bee droppings or excreta.

Fertilize: To make fertile, as by implanting sperm into ova.

Field bees: Bees 2½ to 3 weeks old that collect food for hive.

Flash heater: Device for heating and cooling honey within a few minutes.

Food chamber: Hive body containing honey-filled combs on which bees are expected to live.

Foulbrood: Common name of two brood diseases; usually applied to American foulbrood.

Foundation: *See* Comb foundation.

Frame: Wooden case for holding honeycomb.

Fructose: *See* Levulose.

Fumagillin: Antibiotic given bees to control nosema disease.

Galleria mellonella (L.): Scientific name for greater wax moth.

Giant bee: *See Apis dorsata.*

Glucose: *See* Dextrose.

Grafting: Transfer of larvae from worker cells into queen cells.

Granulated honey: Crystallized or candied honey.

Hive: Man-constructed home for bees.

Hive body: A single wooden rim or shell that holds a set of frames. When used for the brood nest, it is called a brood chamber; when used above the brood nest for honey storage, it is called a super. It may be of various widths and heights and adapted for comb honey sections.

Hive cover: The roof or lid of a hive.

Hive tool: Metal tool for prying supers or frames apart.

Hobbyist beekeeper: One who keeps bees for pleasure or occasional income.

Honey: Sweet viscous fluid elaborated by bees from nectar obtained from plant nectaries, chiefly floral.

Honey bee: Genus *Apis*, family Apidae, order Hymenoptera.

Honey extractor: *See* Extractor.

Honey flow: Period when bees are collecting nectar from plants in plentiful amounts.

Honey house: Building in which honey is extracted and handled.

Honey pump: Pump for transferring liquid honey from one container to another.

Honey stomach: Area inside bee abdomen between esophagus and true stomach.

Honey sump: Temporary honey-holding area with baffles; tends to hold back sizeable pieces of wax and comb.

Honeycomb: Comb built by honey bees with hexagonal back-to-back cells on median midrib.

Honeydew: Sweet secretion from aphids and scale insects.

House bee: A young worker bee, one day to two weeks old, that works only in the hive.

Hybrid bees: The offspring resulting from crosses of two or more selected inbred lines (strains) of bees; the offspring of crosses between races of bees.

Hymenoptera: Order to which all bees belong, as well as ants, wasps, hornets, and yellow jackets.

Inbreeding: A breeding system that features mating of related individuals.

Inner cover: A thin wooden hive lid used beneath a telescoping cover.

Introducing cage: Small wooden and wire cage used to ship queens and also to release them quietly into cluster.

Invertase: Enzyme produced by bee that speeds inversion of sucrose to glucose and fructose.

Italian bees: Bees originally from Italy; most popular race in the United States.

Langstroth hive: A hive with movable frames made possible by the bee space around them. It was invented by L.L. Langstroth.

Larva: Stage in life of bee between egg and pupa; "grub" stage.

Laying worker: Worker bee that lays eggs after colony has been queenless for many days.

Levulose: Fructose or fruit sugar; one of sugars, with glucose, into which sucrose is changed.

Mandibles: Jaws of insects.

Mating flight: Flight taken by virgin queen when she mates with drones in air.

Metamorphosis: Changes of insect from egg to adult.

Migratory beekeeping: Movement of apiaries from one area to another to take advantage of honey flows from different crops.

Movable frame: Frame bees are not inclined to attach to hive because it allows proper bee space around it.

Nectar: Sweet exudate from nectaries of plants.

Nectaries: Special cells in plants from which nectar exudes.

Nosema disease: Disease of bees caused by protozoan spore-forming parasite, *Nosema apis* Zander.

Nuc: Abbreviation for nucleus.

Nuc box: A small hive used for housing a small colony or nucleus.

Nucleus (nuclei): Miniature hives.

Nurse bees: Young worker bees that feed larvae.

Observation hive: Hive with glass sides so that bees can be observed.

Ocellus (ocelli): Simple eye(s) of bees.

Package bees: Screen wire and wood container with live bees, sold by weight of net contents.

Paradichlorobenzene (PDB): A white crystalline substance used to fumigate combs and to repel wax moths.

Parthenogenesis: Production of offspring from virgin female.

Pfund color grader: An instrument used to classify the color of samples of honey.

Pheromone: Chemicals secreted by animals to convey information to or affect behavior of other animals of same species.

Play flight: Short orientation flight taken by young bees, usually by large numbers at one time and during warm part of day.

Pollen: Dust-like material produced in flower and necessary on stigma of female flower for seed production; also collected in pellets on hindlegs of bees.

Pollen basket: Area on hindleg of bee adapted for carrying pellet of pollen.

Pollen cake: Cake of sugar, water, and pollen or pollen substitute for bee feed.

Pollen substitute: Mixture of water, sugar, and other material, such as soy flour, brewer's yeast, and egg yolk, used for bee feed.

Pollen supplement: Mixture, usually of 6 parts (by weight) pollen, 18 parts soy flour, 16 parts water, and 32 parts sugar.

Pollen trap: Device installed over colony entrance that scrapes pollen from legs of entering bees.

Pollination: Transfer of pollen from male to female element of flower.

Pollinator: Agent that transfers pollen.

Pollinizer: Plant that furnishes pollen for another.

Proboscis: Tongue of bee.

Propolis: Resinous material of plants collected and utilized by bees within hive to close small openings or cover objectionable objects within hive.

Pupa: Stage in life of developing bee between larva and adult.

Queen: Sexually developed female bee.

Queen-cage candy: A firm mixture of powdered sugar and liquid invert sugar used in queen cages as food for the queen and her attendant bees.

Queen cell: Cell in which queen develops.

Queen excluder: Device that lets workers pass through but restricts queen.

Queen rearing: Producing queens.

Queen substance: Material produced from glands in head of queen; has strong effect on colony behavior.

Queenless: Without queen.

Queenright: With queen.

Refractometer: An instrument for measuring the percentage of soluble solids in a solution, designed to read directly in percentage of moisture; used for measuring the percentage of moisture in honey and nectar.

Requeening: Removal of a queen from a colony and the introduction of a new one.

Ripe honey: Honey from which bees have evaporated sufficient moisture so that it contains no more than 18.6% water.

Robbing: Bees of one hive taking honey from another.

Royal jelly: Food secreted by worker bees and placed in queen cells for larval food.

Sacbrood: Minor disease of bees caused by filterable virus.

Scout bee: A field bee that locates new sources of food, water, or propolis, or a new home for a swarm.

Sealed brood: Brood in pupal stage with cells sealed.

Shipping cage: Screen and wood container used to ship bees.

Slumgum: The refuse from melted combs after all or part of the wax is removed.

Skep: Beehive made of straw.

Smoker: Device used to blow smoke on bees to reduce stinging.

Solar wax extractor: Glass-covered box in which wax combs are melted by sun's rays and wax is recovered in cake form.

Spermatheca: Small sac-like area in queen in which sperm is stored.

Sting: Modified ovipositor of female Hymenoptera developed into organ of defense.

Streptococcus pluton: Causative agent of European foulbrood.

Sucrose: Sugar; main solid ingredient of nectar before inversion into other sugars.

Supercedure: Replacement of one queen by another while first is still alive.

Swarm: Natural division of colony of bees.

Tarsas: Fifth segment of bee leg.

Telescoping cover: A hive cover, used with an inner cover, that extends downward several inches on all four sides of hive.

Thorax: Middle part of bee.

Tracheae: Breathing tubes of insects.

Uncapping knife: Knife used to remove honey cell caps so honey can be extracted.

Unite: Combine one colony with another.

Unsealed brood: Brood in egg and larval stages only.

Virgin queen: Unmated queen.

Wax glands: Glands on underside of bee abdomen from which wax is secreted after bee has been gorged with food.

Wax moth: Lepidopterous insect whose larvae destroy wax combs.

Wild bees: Any insects that provision their nests with pollen, but do not store surplus edible honey.

Winter cluster: Closely packed colony of bees in winter.

Wired foundation: Foundation with strengthening wires embedded in it.

Wired frames: Frames with wires holding sheets of foundation in place.

Worker bee: Sexually undeveloped female bee.

Worker egg: Fertilized bee egg.

Index

Other AVI Books

BAKERY TECHNOLOGY & ENGINEERING
2nd Edition   *Matz*

BREEDING FIELD CROPS
2nd Edition   *Poehlman*

CANDY TECHNOLOGY
Alikonis

FLAVOR TECHNOLOGY
Heath

FOOD COLORIMETRY THEORY AND APPLICATIONS
Francis and Clydesdale

FUNDAMENTALS OF ENTOMOLOGY AND PLANT PATHOLOGY
2nd Edition   *Pyenson*

LABORATORY MANUAL FOR ENTOMOLOGY AND PLANT
PATHOLOGY   *Pyenson and Barké*

MODERN PASTRY CHEF
Vols. 1 and 2   *Sultan*

PLANT PHYSIOLOGY IN RELATION TO HORTICULTURE
American Edition   *Bleasdale*

PRACTICAL BAKING
3rd Edition   *Sultan*

SMALL FRUIT CULTURE
5th Edition   *Shoemaker*

SOURCE BOOK FOR FOOD SCIENTISTS
Ockerman

SYMPOSIUM: SWEETENERS
Inglett

VEGETABLE GROWING HANDBOOK
Spittstoesser

WHEAT: PRODUCTION & UTILIZATION
Inglett